Postmodern Pooh

Postmodern Pooh

FREDERICK CREWS

PROFILE BOOKS

First published in Great Britain in 2002 by
Profile Books Ltd
58A Hatton Garden
London EC1N 8LX
www.profilebooks.co.uk

First published in the United States in 2001 by
North Point Press

3 5 7 9 10 8 6 4 2

Printed and bound in Great Britain by
Clays, Bungay, Suffolk

ISBN 1 86197 433 7

TO HER

sine te nihil

"Do you know what A means, little Piglet?"

"No, Eeyore, I don't."

"It means Learning, it means Education, it means all the things that you and Pooh haven't got. That's what A means."

Contents

Preface

A second *Pooh Perplex*, thirty-eight years after the first? Well, why not? The idea has often been urged upon your editor by "fans" of the original *Perplex*—mostly literary academics, of course, who have felt bewildered by the proliferation of cutting-edge critical schools since 1963. Another sprightly methodological survey, focusing on the same classic fiction as before, might be just what the doctor ordered to get us all up to speed with the ever-accelerating march of knowledge in our discipline.

Not every reader, of course, is old enough to remember the stir caused by *The Pooh Perplex*, and fewer still will know how to account for it. Truth to tell, no one was more puzzled than I by the book's overnight success. I was then a struggling assistant professor of English, keenly aware of the ticking tenure clock as I cast about fruitlessly for a project—literary-critical, bibliographical, biblio-critico-historical—

whose timely completion might ensure my permanency at UC-Berkeley. As a stopgap, I adopted the then-familiar plan of compiling a "freshman casebook" of other professors' ruminations on a single body of work, the *Pooh* stories. Little did I suspect that those essays, lively though they doubtless were, would captivate thousands of readers. Apparently, I had underestimated the public's hunger to know the best that was being thought and said in "the groves of academe."

Although the prospect of an updated collection has never been out of your editor's mind, it receded as the seventies succeeded the sixties, to be followed in due course by the eighties and then, inexorably, by the nineties. Casebooks are now rarely adopted in freshman English courses; age and infirmity have taken their toll on my mental agility; and, to be candid, I have been no less mystified by "Post-Colonialism" and "Destruction" and "Queer Chicana Studies" than have other academics trained in the once innovative principles of the New Criticism. I might have been a likelier candidate for studying someone else's updated *Perplex* than for compiling one myself!

Here we are, however, ready to go with an array of stimulating and demanding contributions that every student of literature will, I am sure, be eager to get under his belt. I owe this happy outcome to Princeton's great scholar-critic N. Mack Hobbs. He it was who revived my faith that *Pooh* could still reward inquiry from any critical quarter, even the most arcane; who conceived of an instrumentality for generating completely fresh essays, not already printed ones such as those I had harvested from journals back in 1963; and who, with selfless dedication both to me personally and to the cause of disinterested learning, saw the entire project through to completion. It all came about as follows.

In 1997, when I was on the verge of retiring from forty years of service to my Berkeley department, that unit was vigorously attempting—in vain, I regret to say—to woo the distinguished Professor Hobbs away from Princeton. On recruiting visits, Hobbs made a point of meeting privately with every member of our tenured staff and cordially inquiring into the current state of our research. In my own case, awkwardly, there was nothing to discuss. But, *faute de mieux*, I did press into Hobbs's hand a warmly inscribed copy of *The Pooh Perplex*. He leafed through the book with mounting and barely contained enthusiasm, finally exclaiming, "This is wonderful stuff! Do you know what you've got here, more than three decades before its time? It's Teaching the Conflicts!"

Hobbs went on to explain that Teaching the Conflicts was now all the rage in collegiate literary pedagogy. Previously, majors in English had been lurching haphazardly from one opinionated professor to another, picking up contradictory signals about "the" correct way to interpret, say, *Paradise Regained* or "Elegy Written in a Country Churchyard." But under Teaching the Conflicts, all of those clashes of viewpoint are anticipated and given a curricular function. Today, Hobbs told me, the very disputes that cause professors of literature to defame one another as sexists, fascists, and idiots can become the *organized* heart of the major.

A Teaching-the-Conflicts English department says in effect to expectant nineteen-year-olds—and Hobbs kindly wrote out this baffling lingo at my request—"Here is Husserlian phenomenology, here are the Jungian archetypes, here is Jakobsonian structuralism, here is Zizekian Lacanianism, here is Counterhegemonic Post-Gramscian Marxism, and here is the Deleuzoguattarian Anti-Oedipus; now *you* decide which hermeneutic should prevail." Thus a newly minted B.A. can step confidently into the greater world, not knowing Milton and Gray, perhaps, but knowing exactly how he would want to account for the magic of their art, should the occasion ever arise.

Wasn't that, Hobbs asked, just what I had implicitly proposed in 1963? Apparently so, though I hadn't realized it at the time; *The Pooh Perplex* had anticipated the most advanced thought of the sophisticated nineties. Why not greet the millennium, then, with a completely fresh exemplar of the same project? Hobbs immediately came up with a plan.

He himself, he said, would be attending the Modern Language Association's December 2000 convention in Washington, D.C., and he had already been seeking a panel to chair. Given his international prestige, he could easily solicit methodologically acute papers on *Pooh* from leading figures in our field. And if the draft papers were circulated in advance, the participants would be sure to have usefully conflictual things to say about one another's premises. Moreover, a team of Hobbs's own graduate assistants could see to collecting and editing the papers and preparing the biographical headnotes that would introduce each chapter. All I had to do myself was compose this preface and mail it off to Professor Hobbs.

These proposals were so handsome that I hesitated before making one request of my own. Still a bit uncomfortable with the novelty of deliberately fomenting "conflict," I asked whether Hobbs could include in the panel a social and cultural critic whom I especially admire, Dudley Cravat III. I knew that if any other presenter were to stray into incivility,

Cravat would be the man to steer the assembled company back to a duly literary atmosphere. Hobbs graciously acceded to my plea. Though Cravat, as a nonmember, was technically ineligible to join an MLA forum, Hobbs assured me that *he* would be making up the rules for this panel.

As of this writing, your editor of record hasn't yet seen the full text that both he and you will soon be savoring. I have been assured by Professor Hobbs, however, that the Washington conference matched or exceeded all of his expectations. My only regret is that I was too frail to "make the scene" in person and hear the warm tributes to *The Pooh Perplex* that were doubtless voiced by Hobbs and others.

But there is one further disappointment to report. I had hoped that this volume, like its predecessor, would be graced by illustrations from the *Pooh* books. To my surprise, however, Professor Hobbs has informed me that permission for that use was denied by Dutton Children's Books and the Trustees of the Pooh Properties. Why, I wonder? Surely a classic of juvenile literature has nothing to fear from a fresh generation of scholarly knights riding off in quest of image patterns, paradoxes, and mythic parallels. And even if those worthies have ventured into yet more exotic forests of polysignification and organic form, what of that? Each uncovered nuance will only have added a leaf to the garland crowning the brow of the Best Bear in All the World.

My first hypothesis, when I heard the distressing news about the pictures, was that there must now be a uniform policy forbidding any reuse of Ernest H. Shepard's drawings. A glance at *Books in Print*, however, disabused me of that notion. The very publishing house that seems to have found *Postmodern Pooh* objectionable has employed Shepard's work to adorn *Pooh's Little Coloring Book*, *Baby's First Winnie-the-Pooh*, *Eeyore Has a Birthday*, *Tigger's Giant Lift-the-Flap Book*, *Pooh's Little Etiquette Book*, and *Eeyore's Gloomy Little Instruction Book*, along with a number of adult titles such as *The Tao of Pooh*, *The Te of Piglet*, *Pooh and the Philosophers*, *Winnie-the-Pooh on Management*, and *Winnie-the-Pooh on Problem Solving*. Each publication, I feel sure, meets a pressing social need. But what, then, about the needs of college students adrift on the choppy, horizonless seas of literary interpretation?

May I close on a frankly autobiographical note? *Postmodern Pooh* forms a bookend, as it were, concluding my long if uneventful career of devotion both to humanistic values and to *Pooh*. And are they really so different, one from the other? The bright critics assembled in this volume will doubtless show, in their sophisticated and ingenious new ways, that just as *Pooh* is suffused with humanism, our humanism itself, by this late date, has become full of *Pooh*. On that one point, at least, I feel certain that no "conflict" is likely to emerge.

Frederick Crews
Berkeley, California

Postmodern Pooh

CHAPTER ONE

Why? Wherefore?
Inasmuch as Which?

FELICIA MARRONNEZ

Felicia Marronnez is Sea & Ski Professor of English at the University of California at Irvine. All of her degrees, however, were awarded by Yale University, and it was from Yale's English department that she relocated to Irvine in 1990, with the specific aim of helping to narrow the sophistication gap between our two coasts. In view of her prizewinning dissertation, "Heidegger Reading *Pooh* Reading Hegel Reading Husserl: Or, Isn't It Punny How a Hun Likes Beary?," Marronnez has been well situated to demonstrate how the ethically serious Derrideanism of the Yale school illuminates the subtleties of the *Pooh* books. That promise was fully realized in her subsequent monograph, *(P)ooh La La! Kiddie Lit Gets the Jacques of Its Life* (Yale University Press, 1992).

"Well," said Pooh, "we keep looking for Home and not finding it, so I thought that if we looked for this Pit, we'd be sure not to find it, which would be a Good Thing, because then we might find something that we *weren't* looking for, which might be just what we *were* looking for, really."

ONE might say that the reader who has grasped the full significance of this passage has seen to the bottom of both *Winnie-the-Pooh* and its author. Yes, one might say that. But "one" would thereby be branded as a simpleton, a theory-starved dunce. "Grasped the full significance"? "Seen to the bottom"? Not very likely.

Pooh, it's true, manages, through byzantine byways that I will track below, to body forth the key principles of Deconstruction with uncanny fidelity. And that fact, given the apparent temporal priority of Milne over Derrida, would seem to prove the timeless pertinence of the latter's approach to textuality. Yet what is the *leçon* of Derrida, that consummate rhetor of the iterable and the dehiscent, if not that clear sight, the grasping of significance, and even historical precedence (to say nothing of timeless truth) are all illusions, effects of that very *différance* that constitutes the only legitimate object of critical scrutiny?

I wonder how many of you went for my feint that we might learn something here about the author of *Winnie-the-Pooh*. *C'est pour rire*. Pooh Bear, at least, knows better:

> I sometimes wonder if it's true
> That who is what and what is who.

After all, J. Hillis Miller has pointed out that "there is not any 'Shakespeare himself,'"[1] and Derrida once observed that "there is not, strictly speaking, a text whose author or subject is Jean-Jacques Rousseau."[2] It's fairly clear, then, that Miller is right when he characterizes *every* author as merely "an effect of the text."[3] "A. A. Milne" himself or itself concedes the point in the preface to *When We Were Very Young*:

> You may wonder sometimes who is supposed to be saying the verses. Is it the Author, that strange but uninteresting person, or is it Christopher Robin, or some other boy or girl, or Nurse, or Hoo? . . . you will have to decide for yourselves.

As for "the reader," spare me! The term elides difference, attempts to inscribe on a bubbling bouillabaisse of potentialities one model of a stolid, passive, tabula rasa receptor. Grant yourself a "reader" and you automatically become a *writer*—worse, a *communicator* with a plain *message* that "the reader" will supposedly open like some ersatz telegram announcing that he has been declared a finalist in the Publishers Clearing House Sweepstakes.

Now that we've dispensed with both author and reader, you will be interested to learn that I'm going to go right on discussing them. And the same holds for both truth and

---

1. J. Hillis Miller, "Ariachne's Broken Woof," *Georgia Review* 30 (Spring 1976), p. 59.

2. Jacques Derrida, *Of Grammatology*, trans. Gayatri Chakravorty Spivak (Baltimore and London: Johns Hopkins Univ. Press, 1976), p. 246.

3. Miller, "Ariachne's Broken Woof," p. 59.

literary meaning, notions at once fallacious and essential to the work of Deconstruction. After we have registered the fatal instability of our concepts, they still remain *our concepts*, all the more precious for our awareness that they, and therefore we, fail to intersect with "reality" at any point. As *Pooh* shows in numerous ways, we cannot do otherwise than yearn for unwobbling transcendence, especially when we see it dissolving into linguistic supplement and remainder.

Think of the scene in which Winnie-the-Pooh, supposedly on a purposeful march to call on his friends, pauses squarely in the middle of an entropic stream. Oblivious of its unilinear flow toward oblivion, slack-jawed Pooh, stubby arms at perfect rest on beloved belly, sits on a rock as solid as the one Dr. Johnson kicked to refute Berkeley. Using a passing dragonfly as a quadrant, he aims his nose straight at the warming sun. Heliotrope: that is Derrida's stunning metaphor for our arching toward the Logos, source of all the false light by which we (think we) "discern the significance," "see things in perspective," "apply the light of common sense," or "develop a vision."

Pooh's eyes, however, are closed. Paunchy Panza, catching the rays *without reflection*. He seeks nothing, perceives nothing, propounds nothing, but merely sings the noncommittally conditional, innocently egoistic "I could spend a happy morning / Being Pooh."

Being—*Dasein*! What is Pooh in this tableau if not the personification (ursification?) of Man stripped of all striving, truly attuned, for once, to that discursive impossibility, a Nature without cultural excess or archive? No dispersal here, no deferral or dissemination. But look what happens next:

The sun was so delightfully warm, and the stone, which had been sitting in it for a long time, was so warm, too, that Pooh had almost decided to go on being Pooh in the middle of the stream for the rest of the morning, when he remembered Rabbit.

"When he remembered Rabbit." Rabbit the nosy busybody, the restless, envious brain, the all-around expert who always gets it wrong. Rabbit is *discourse itself*, particularly in its most seductively "present" form, speech. And though Pooh never wants anything from Rabbit but food, it is no coincidence that the act-ivation of his bodily need co-insides with the prospect of his vulnerability to the *Pooh* books' most logorrheic talker. There is no free lunch, not even in the sacred forest of childhood. Once having felt a pang, we can gain our sustenance only by becoming dealers and supplicants within the web of signifiers, that differential network of traces both producing and exceeding "meaning" without ever duplicating the object of desire.

Now we can discern why Pooh, in Rabbit's company somewhat later, gets "into a comfortable position for not listening to Rabbit." Here he attunes himself, defensively, to gentle forest sounds "which all seemed to be saying to Pooh, 'Don't listen to Rabbit, listen to me.'" But Rabbit, of course, prevails, and Pooh is swept from trance into transaction yet again. To submit to Rabbit is to be drawn into the "present" as it attempts to "be itself," the advancing edge of nervous conative (go native?) will. Pooh, however, doesn't have to like it. He senses—or rather, we sense through him—the speciousness of such contemporaneity. As Derrida—drawing from what Seán Burke has called his "*apparatus criticus* . . . awesome in its relentless invagination"[4]—points out:

> An interval must separate the present from what it is
> not in order for the present to be itself, but this interval
> that constitutes it as present must, by the same token,
> divide the present in and of itself, thereby also divid-
> ing, along with the present, everything that is
> thought on the basis of the present, that is, in our
> metaphysical language, every being, and singularly
> substance or the subject.[5]

Some auditors, I know, will consider this line of inquiry a bit too theoretical for their taste. That's a pity, but Hillis Miller and the late Paul de Man proved long ago that Deconstruction, reading, and theory are all exactly the same thing. If you attempt to reject that conclusion, you will only be generating more theory and thus illustrating Paul's law. Hillis put it succinctly in his famous, feisty presidential address to the MLA: "If the resistance to theory is the resistance to reading, theory is itself the resistance to theory, therefore a resistance to the reading it advocates."[6]

Although all literary works, when rigorously analyzed, yield what Paul de Man called "allegories of the impossibility

4. Seán Burke, *The Death and Return of the Author: Criticism and Subjectivity in Barthes, Foucault, and Derrida*, 2nd ed. (Edinburgh: Edinburgh Univ. Press, 1998), p. 144.

5. Jacques Derrida, *Margins of Philosophy*, trans. Alan Bass (Chicago: Univ. of Chicago Press, 1982), p. 13.

6. J. Hillis Miller, Presidential Address, 1986: "The Triumph of Theory, the Resistance to Reading, and the Question of the Material Base," *PMLA* 102 (1987), p. 286.

of reading,"[7] the ethics of Deconstruction require that we favor the "strong misreading" instead of the "weak misreading."[8] We wouldn't want to claim, for example, that *Winnie-the-Pooh* is really about the U.S. Patent Office, America Online, or Fermat's last theorem. Instead, we must first establish what the text is "trying to say," so that we can then go about discovering its antiphonal, antipodal antiself. In *Pooh*'s case, that manifest theme is the need to practice tolerant sociability—a virtue that supposedly redeems the protagonist's near absence of gray matter. But is that fixed intention of "A. A. Milne's" realized without breaching, effraction, or polylogue? Deconstructors, start your engines!

Attend to Pooh without sentimentality and ask yourself what positive social traits he can plausibly be taken to represent. He is a freeloader whose affability extends no further than his next honey fix. Deconstructed, he is just a mouth and a digestive tract in charge of some rudimentary powers of rationalization. And when he is confronted with a different genus (the apian) pursuing its own programmed livelihood, he shows himself utterly incapable of acknowledging the Other. "The only reason for making honey," he deduces with infantile self-in-*fat*-uation, "is so as *I* can eat it." Community values? One for all and all for one?

Furthermore, Pooh's selfishness is no greater than that of the whole kapok menagerie surrounding him. It is only his inability to disguise or dignify raw need that renders him the touchstone of value-in-reverse. While the hidebound "Milne"

---

7. Paul de Man, *Allegories of Reading: Figural Language in Rousseau, Nietzsche, Rilke, and Proust* (New Haven: Yale Univ. Press, 1979), p. 205.
8. J. Hillis Miller, "Deconstructing the Deconstructors," *Diacritics* 5 (Summer 1978), p. 24.

is musing complacently about rectitude and cooperation, his principal creation embodies a brute-all Brechtian forthrightness about the priority of aliment over intellect—and therefore of his majesty the ego over moral claims. Every gregarious sentiment in these books stands self-refuted in the very act of articulation.

Consider also that the enchanted forest is presided over by the seeming child-god Christ-opher Robin, who, from the animals' occluded point of view, is assumed to be utterly loyal and attentive to them. As we progress toward the dissonant climax of *The House at Pooh Corner*, however, it becomes increasingly apparent that Christopher is coming under the thrall of that deadly Pied Piper, Western culture. His mind will soon be warped by the lexical and calculative disciplinary—that is, by spelling and math—imparted, no doubt, with the mnemonic aid of thwacks from a sadistic schoolmaster's ruler, its numbingly identical spaces marked off with vertical lines forming a lockstep zombie parade of Baconian/Newtonian "units." During his ever more frequent absences, we can infer, he is becoming just the sort of know-it-all bore lampooned in the pushy schemer Rabbit and the insufferable pedant Owl. The text, chewing away like an army of termites beneath "Milne's" conscious mind, has included those ridiculous "intellectuals" precisely in order to facilitate our strong misreading.

Is this at last, then, the "meaning" of *Winnie-the-Pooh*: the falseness of every overtly proffered ideal? If you suppose so, I want you to listen carefully from here on. A strong misreading is still a *reading*, with all its loose ends tucked neatly out of sight. Since meaning, as one of "Milne's" poems proclaims, "isn't really anywhere! / It's somewhere else instead," the meaning of nonmeaning must itself be deconstructed if we are to keep pace with the text's self-dissolution.

Jonathan Culler once memorably defined this task for us. A critic's role, he wrote, is that of "sawing off the branch on which one is sitting":

> One can and may continue to sit on a branch while sawing it. There is no physical or moral obstacle if one is willing to risk the consequences. The question then becomes whether one will succeed in sawing it clear through, and where and how one might land. A difficult question: to answer one would need a comprehensive understanding of the entire situation—the resilience of the support, the efficacy of one's tools, the shape of the terrain—and an ability to predict accurately the consequences of one's work.[9]

Note, here, how Culler, much in the spirit of Pooh and Piglet carefully pondering how best to trap a Heffalump, eschews premature closure. Just what will happen when the branch is severed remains a topic of meticulously—perhaps even permanently—postponed investigation.

The branch on which we wielders of critical discourse sit is logocentrism: the assumption, both delusory and irreplaceable, that the signifiers we employ actually denote their signified objects, nothing more or less. But the *Pooh* books continually saw away at that very premise. "This writing business," as Eeyore puts it. "Pencils and what-not.

---

9. Jonathan Culler, *On Deconstruction: Theory and Criticism after Structuralism* (Ithaca: Cornell Univ. Press, 1982), p. 149.

Over-rated, if you ask me. Silly stuff. Nothing in it." Naturally, Eeyore does not mean to challenge Derrida's point that language in general is just a special case of writing. Quite the contrary: he perceives, as does Derrida, that writing as a direct conveyor of meaning, with necessary connections between word and object, begs to be devalued. By ascribing this lesson to Eeyore, the text implies that any ass could learn it.

It is, once again, the emergent pupil Christopher Robin, the apple-polishing regurgitator of potted "facts," whose stock declines in direct seesaw linkage with the uncerebral Eeyore's rise. By comparison with Milne's pampered but incipiently regimented offspring, even the numskull Pooh, whose mouth remains in readiness at all moments for regression from emitting speech to ingesting snacks, appears deeply wise. Indeed, he sounds on occasion like a shrewd postanalytic philosopher: "You find sometimes that a Thing [*ein Ding*] which seemed very Thingish [*dinglich*] inside you is quite different [*différent/différant*] when it gets out into the open and has other people looking at it."

Not only Pooh in the flesh but *Pooh* as a text habitually concretizes social constructs, reversing the sinister process whereby mere things were once promoted to signifiers. You may have thought that the North Pole, for example, means something as abstract as latitude 90° and longitude 0°, but for *Pooh* it's just a stick in the ground. Other sticks appear to constitute Eeyore's house, which is then disassembled, only to rematerialize as the very same house. But *is* it the same, plunked down on an alien plot? Here the text, with Heraclitean panache, puts into question self-identity itself, the principle lying behind all Western thought from Plato through Husserl.

Again, it is noteworthy that Owl's letter box, rendered useless for its original logocentric function, serves as the escape hatch through which Piglet emerges to become, himself, a parodic incarnate missive. Derrida's recurrent pun, in *La carte postale*, between *l'être* and *lettre*, showing that Being can never be captured in language, echoes in our minds throughout the episode. The postcard, you will recall, is Derrida's image for the modern world's fondest illusion:

> Everything in our bildopedic culture, in our politics of the encyclopedic, in our telecommunications of all genres, in our telematicometaphysical archives . . . everything is constructed on the protocolary charter of an axiom, that could be demonstrated, displayed on a large *carte*, a post card of course, since it is so simple, elementary, a brief, fearful stereotyping.[10]

If you catch the heavy irony here—the culture of "communication" rests on the fib that signifiers can make their way from one party to another with no fading or twisting of informational content—you will see why *Pooh* reduces the standard literary notion of rescue (that is, salvation) to a self-mailed postcard consisting of a timid little pig. Having a wonderful time, wish you were oink oink oink.

A still more suggestive torpedoing of the communicative, however, makes use of the bellpull adorning the marge or limen of Owl's tree house. Ostensibly, that object serves as a sign of the querulous bird's (distinctly tepid and equivocal)

---

10. Jacques Derrida, *The Post Card: From Socrates to Freud and Beyond*, trans. Alan Bass (Chicago and London: Univ. of Chicago Press, 1987), p. 20.

hospitality. Yet once deconstructed, it reveals itself to be nothing other than Eeyore's missing tail, which, if you stop to think about it in anatomical context, can't be said to constitute a fetching invitation to give a pull and begin speaking into the intercom. As usual, Derrida has said it all: "That the sign *detaches itself*, that signifies of course that one *cuts it out of its place of emission* or from its natural relations; but the separation is never perfect, the difference never consummated."[11]

Since you now know that a detached sign is precisely a name without a referent, you can appreciate why much of the text's deconstructive satire is focused on the problematic status of names. When Pooh is, quite literally, living "under the name of Sanders," he finds himself in possession not of yet another alias but of a mere board with some misshapen scratchings on it. Graphemically aleatory and semioclastic, it is a sign without meaning. To go in search of the mythical Sanders, just because the indentations on that board bear an uncanny resemblance to the letters S-A-N-D-E-R-S, would thus be as quixotic as trying to locate the beheaded or castrated William of "TRESPASSERS W." The text instructs us not to bother; (S)anders is the ever-deferred Other (*anders*), or (non)personhood per se, our doppelgänger whose face is always turned aside.

If the sign of all signs is the name, the most "authentic" of names is the signature. But suppose the signature were to surrender its claim to vouch for the seamless self and instead be unmasked as just so much extruded ink. No one then, I

---

11. Jacques Derrida, *Glas* (Paris: Editions Galilee, 1974), p. 88; emphasis added.

daresay, could fail to grant that the literary work embodying such logodefusion has embarked on Derrida's own most urgent project—in his words, "to paralyze the signature's sperm."[12] Well, do you recall the eight signatures deposited on Eeyore's farewell poem to Christopher Robin? Six characters (in search of an author?) more or less succeed in spelling their names, but the sequence ends explosively with Tigger's inarticulate *BLOT* and Roo's even more diffuse *SMUDGE*, as if to say to the others, *Scribble away if you must, but in the end it comes to this.*

There is, of course, a political as well as a semiotic lesson here. *Pooh* is trying to say that nothing short of a thorough-going revolt against the equivalence of word and thing, name and person, signature and certification can overcome the stifling of our prelinguistic freedom. A comparable insight enabled Derrida to show that South African apartheid, which some dull analysts had blamed on a tenacious and fearful white minority, was actually brought about by phonetic writing, which, "by isolating and hypostatizing being, . . . corrupts it into a quasi-ontological segregation."[13] Apartheid has vanished now, so we can safely conclude that South African phonetic writing must be in full retreat. The only mystery is why the Nobel Peace Prize went to the prosaic literalist Nelson Mandela and not to Derrida.

Well, that is water under the Poohsticks bridge. The good news is that from Johns Hopkins to Johannesburg, from Sewanee to Soweto, people are confirming Hillis Miller's joyous prophecy that "the millennium would come if all men

---

12. Derrida, *Glas*, p. 280.
13. Jacques Derrida, "Racism's Last Word," *Critical Inquiry* 12 (1985), p. 292.

and women became good readers in de Man's sense."[14] Wherever we turn, furthermore, we find less and less of what Geoffrey Hartman once deplored as "the automatic valuing of works of art over works of commentary."[15] Now it seems to be generally accepted that while fictions—including *Pooh*, of course—all mean pretty much the same thing, deconstructive criticism can be infinitely various and creative.

It can also be wild and freakish fun. Since "the absence of the transcendental signified extends the domain and the interplay of signification *ad infinitum*,"[16] critics are thereby freed to practice what Hartman calls "Derridadaism,"[17] a "methodical craziness" or "vertiginous *glissement* of language toward an uncontrollable echoing; a mad round of verbal associations of signifier-signifying signifiers."[18] As Gregory Ulmer explains, "The idea put to work hypomnemically . . . is not the signified concept . . . but the letters/phonemes of the word itself, which are set free to generate conceptual material *mechanically* (without the intention or presence of the subject) by gathering into a discourse terms possessing these letters."[19]

---

14. J. Hillis Miller, *The Ethics of Reading: Kant, de Man, Eliot, Trollope, James, and Benjamin* (New York: Columbia Univ. Press, 1987), p. 58.

15. Geoffrey H. Hartman, *Criticism in the Wilderness: The Study of Literature Today* (New Haven: Yale Univ. Press, 1980), p. 103.

16. Jacques Derrida, "Structure, Sign, and Play in the Discourse of the Human Sciences," in *The Structuralist Controversy*, ed. Richard Macksey and Eugenio Donato (Baltimore: Johns Hopkins Univ. Press, 1970), p. 249.

17. Geoffrey H. Hartman, *Saving the Text: Literature/Derrida/Philosophy* (Baltimore: Johns Hopkins Univ. Press, 1981), p. 33.

18. Hartman, *Saving the Text*, pp. 62, 111.

19. Gregory L. Ulmer, *Applied Grammatology: Post(e)-Pedagogy from Jacques Derrida to Joseph Beuys* (Baltimore: Johns Hopkins Univ. Press, 1985), p. 65.

We Derridadaists are behind the *whee*-l now, swerving with verve to avoid the pedestrian. If a Woozle can Wizzle, so can I. This little Piglet went to mark it; will he Roo the day? "*Sériature* of *sériature*: antherection, *colpos*, signature, stewke, betweens, *colossos*."[20] Cottleston, Cottleston, Pie in your eye. HIPY PAPY BTHUTHDTH THUTHDA BTHUTHDY!

---

20. John P. Leavey, Jr., *GLASsary* (Lincoln: Univ. of Nebraska Press, 1986), p. 122.

CHAPTER TWO

A Bellyful of Pooh

VICTOR S. FASSELL

Arriving at Stanford with Ph.D. in hand at the remarkably fresh age of twenty-four, Victor Fassell soon began making an indelible mark on literary criticism. From the day that his precocious article of 1972, "*Dick* Description: The Codpiece as Signifier, Fetish, and Symbolic Actor," was published in *Glyph*, he distinguished himself as one of the young American critics to be most closely watched and emulated. Quite by accident, in fact, he became the reluctant leader of an entire movement. As Fassell wryly recounted somewhat later, a phrase that he had casually tossed into an essay about the curious mutuality between Vasco da Gama and the viola da gamba got picked up and mistaken for some sort of battle cry. Before long, despite Fassell's attempts to discourage them, legions of academics in various fields were rallying to a critical school he had never meant to found, "The New— *All*-New!—Negotiationism."

Fassell's books include *The Sorcerer's Appendix: Early Modern Medicine and the Alchemy of the Sonnet*; *Royal Pain: The Hemorrhoidal Imagination in the Court of Queen Anne*; and, most recently, his study of the conjunction between everyday life and supernatural belief, *Incredible Banality*. Founder and former editor of the trendsetting journal *Quelconque*, he has assumed the general editorship of two ambitious new series, Routledge's The All-New Negotiationists and McGraw-Hill's The Assigned Textbook.

In 1998, after a fierce bidding war among several institutions, Professor Fassell joined the faculty of Rice University, where he now holds the coveted Exxon Valdez Chair in the Humanities.

ACCORDING to a prophecy announced by two Reformed Seventh-Day Adventists, Robert Reidt and Margaret Rowen, the world as it was then known would reach a spectacular end on February 6, 1925—just one year before the publication, across the turbulent but no more than usually agitated Atlantic Ocean, of *Winnie-the-Pooh*. If Reidt and Rowen were correctly apprised of the divine plan, the whole population of planet Earth would be annihilated except for 144,000 worshipful penitents, who would take a brief respite on Jupiter during their seven-day ascent to heaven. *A fortiori*, there would be nobody left down here to appreciate a never-to-be completed work of fiction from the pen of A. A. Milne, whose name was evidently missing from the roll of the Remnant.

Adventist seers had been wrong before—indeed, with monotonous regularity—and, as you may already have surmised, once again their calculations proved to be off the mark. At 11:55 p.m. on February 6, Reidt inspected the unremarkable sky and conceded, "Well, it doesn't look as if anything is going to happen tonight." Yet this, too, was spoken in error. At that very hour, availing himself of an amnesty bill recently passed by the national legislature in Paris, a French army deserter turned himself in. It was the famous socialite Suzanne Langlard, whose real name was Paul Grappe. Grappe pronounced himself delighted with the amnesty because, he confided, he had grown tired of wearing women's clothes.[1]

Jupiter is nowhere mentioned in the *Pooh* books, but neither, for that matter, is Grappe/Langlard. It doesn't prove a thing, one way or the other. Suggestive at least is the fact that Jupiter, as the foremost polymorphously perverse seducer among the Olympian gods, was by no means above engaging in some cross-dressing of his own. As I hardly need to point out, the same can be said of that baby-kangaroo impersonator Piglet, in *The House at Pooh Corner*. Moreover, Jupiter and his fellow immortals engaged in much dissolute tippling, to which the noncognominal initials of our author, "A.A.," might well be taken to stand as an implied rebuke. At a minimum, there is food for thought here. Conclusions beckon flickeringly from the middle distance, even if they disdain to be roughly seized and pocketed in the crass style of traditionalist criticism.

Apropos of predecessor movements, let me pause here to say how pleased I am to be speaking not only in Washington—

---

1. See Cate Plys, "A Brief History of the End of Time," *Washington City Paper*, June 24, 1994, p. 18.

which has made quite an impressive recovery, I must say, since it was sacked by the British in 1814—but also on the same platform as Felicia Marronnez, whom I've run across at many a prior conference from Bellagio to Prague to Dar es Salaam. She has just performed a commendable feat of time travel, wafting us back to the heady days when Derrideans called the academic shots.

It's no fault of Professor Marronnez's that Deconstruction dwindled so rapidly after Paul de Man's posthumous disgrace, which she chose not to mention today. "Neither Derrida nor de Man has ever sequestered his enterprise from politics or history," Hillis Miller had declared in his notorious MLA presidential address. Well, yes and no. While Hitler's fortunes were still in the ascendant, the young Belgian journalist de Man made no secret of his Nazi sympathies, but a certain reticence set in thereafter. Deconstructive "undecidability" took on a darker coloration when the full story came to light. Even de Man, however, couldn't have wrecked Deconstruction all by himself. The movement imploded only when Professor Marronnez's other idols, the chief surviving proponents of "misreading," began complaining, farcically, that their beloved friend's collaborationist prose from the 1940s was being "misread."

By now, fortunately, some of us who stand rather to the left of de Man and Derrida have shown how an expanded close reading—not willful misreading—can bring into view the subtle interplay, or *negotiation*, between literary art and the specific energies that recycle through an age. We've shown that works such as *Pooh* don't drift toward a banal meaninglessness; they become active historical players in their own right, shaping the public's illusions about the important issues of the day, such as conquistadorial predation, witch trials, *ius primae noctis*, and the castration of preadolescent countertenors. Though these are not precisely the major themes of *Pooh*, vigilance against their resuscitation in modern texts would be prudent, given our new awareness that literature feeds directly into policy at the highest levels of power.

Take, for example, the abdication of Edward VIII from the British throne in 1936. England's privy councillors could hardly have failed to note that at the end of *The House at Pooh Corner*, Edward Bear is granted a knighthood as a means of bidding him good riddance. Was the ruling class emboldened to demote the King to Duke of Windsor by the example of that earlier Edward, an even bigger ninny than the monarch? And had the future royal dropout been subliminally primed for abdication by verses like these?

They're changing guard at Buckingham Palace— . . .
We looked for the King, but he never came.

My questions admit of no ready answers. But if, as other students of socioliterary negotiations have shown, a court pageant sank the Spanish Armada; if *Macbeth* prompted the introduction of sanitary controls over soup ingredients; if the outcome of the Battle of Antietam was determined by martial themes in Emily Dickinson; and if Wordsworth's poetry brought about a speculative boom in daffodil futures, then surely these modest hypotheses ought not to be dismissed out of hand.

In physique, of course, Pooh calls to mind not the Duke of Windsor but his Tory detractor Winston Churchill—

himself much given to snacking and napping at unorthodox hours. Moreover, Churchill was already prominent, indeed controversial, when Milne sat down to compose those tales whose artfulness compels our grudging praise even as we necessarily resist their ideological seduction. Churchill had achieved notoriety in the Great War of 1914–1918 when, at Gallipoli, he courted disaster by deploying an indispensable portion of the Royal Navy in a before-the-fact game of Pooh-sticks. Under the assumptions of a bygone era, a critic might have been inclined to call Pooh "a Churchill figure" and have done with it. But now we can carry the inquiry forward and ask to what extent the British role in the second general war, that of 1939–1945, may have been at once prefigured in and molded by Winston's—Winnie's!—exposure, as a well-read parliamentarian, to all those stiff-upper-lip doings in that anti-Berchtesgaden, Milne's enchanted forest, where cries for *Lebensraum* would surely have fallen on deaf ears.

Given their uncanny physical resemblance, it seems fair to say that both Pooh and Churchill profited, in their social dealings, from arctophilia, or love of bears. That this was nothing new may be instanced by the fact that Lord Byron, as an undergraduate, had kept a rescued performing bear in his rooms at Cambridge. Moreover, anyone who doubts that the same sympathy was alive and well in 1926 need only consult the 1924 trial record of Leopold and Loeb, the nineteen-year-old American murderers of young Bobby Franks, who were spared the death penalty when a defense psychiatrist convinced the judge that Loeb was "still a little child emotionally, still talking to his teddy bear."

Foucault has shown that phenomena come into existence only when they are named within a discourse. Consider, for example, the dark continent of the human armpits, which remained unexplored, because unidentified as any kind of place at all, until the marketing of deodorants began just around the time of *Pooh*. Not soon enough, however, for the trickle-down effect, as it were, to bring the axillae into meaningful focus in that text. The question then arises, naturally, whether the body itself existed for A. A. Milne. Or, thanks to his sheltered upbringing and the general sway of repression over the English mind, was it simply unthinkable?

To begin inching toward an answer, I will focus on the salient but never critically remarked fact that all of the characters in *Pooh* except Christopher Robin—who looks, wouldn't you agree, rather like Twiggy in shrunken shorts—are stark naked. (The other apparent clothes wearer, Piglet, is no exception; what looks at first like a cutaway wet suit proves on closer inspection to be a fanciful assemblage of pork rinds, or second skin.) One apron briefly appearing on Kanga's bosom and one ribbon on Eeyore's tail, instead of contradicting my point, only serve to underscore it by fetishizing the breast and the phallus, respectively—as would, for example, such appurtenances as pasties, a G-string, or a penile plethysmograph, this last being employed forensically, as is well known, to judge exactly what does and doesn't arouse an accused sex offender. Eeyore's ribbon makes just such an impression on a critic who is not afraid to follow analogies wherever they may lead.

The immediate issue here is whether the *Pooh* animals realize that they constitute a de facto nudist colony. If not, this can only mean that Milne himself must have banished that awareness to his unconscious. Furthermore, we must ask why Ernest Shepard's drawings, which were surely subject to the author's review, deprived these exemplars of the tiger, the bear, the rabbit, the pig, the kangaroo, and the owl of overtly rendered genitalia. Since the jungle and the barnyard have never been known as loci of prudery, suspicion must fall once again on the human subject Milne, who, at the very height of the Jazz Age, appears to have been registering an otherwise unnoticed shift of episteme that would, in time, eventuate in the massive desexualization typified in such antiseptic figures as Margaret Thatcher, Kenneth Starr, and Barney the Dinosaur.

There is always a chance, however, that the *Pooh* characters, despite the way in which such husky-voiced pronouns as *he*, *him*, and *his* wistfully cling to most of them, suffer from gender uncertainty if not from outright hermaphroditism. If so, they surely allude ironically to the case of Marie le Marcis, the young chambermaid from Rouen who in 1601 represented herself as a man with a hidden penis, thereby rebuffing the criminal charge that she had committed sodomy with her female lover. Marie's alleged member was nothing but a clitoris, which the obtuse examining physician, Jacques Duval, deemed distinctively male though not much to write home about. The jury, however, was satisfied, and the acquitted Marie passed her remaining days in freedom, prudently disguised as a bearded tailor. She continued her dalliances with women but, needless to say, never became a lesbian, because that term wasn't yet in currency.[2]

If the reader doubts that a problematic surrounding both nudity and sexual identity is at play in *Pooh*, let me invite renewed scrutiny of the scene in which Piglet, having been at

---

2. See Katharine Park, "The Rediscovery of the Clitoris: French Medicine and the Tribade, 1570–1620," in *The Body in Parts: Fantasies of Corporeality in Early Modern Europe*, ed. David Hillman and Carla Mazzio (New York and London: Routledge, 1997), pp. 171–93.

once infantilized, sanitized, and marsupialized by Kanga, the sadistic foster mother, escapes and seizes the first opportunity to reassert his porcine nature. When safely close to his house, "he stopped running, and rolled the rest of the way home, so as to get his own nice comfortable colour again. . . ." Given the linguistic nexus among *propre*, *propriety*, and *property*, we may here observe that Piglet, quite literally (re)making a pig of himself, is attempting to reap*propr*iate his swinishness by means of caking his torso in topsoil and the refuse that it entails. The move appears quixotic, in that a nominal remasculinization (dirt=sex) places a virtual fig leaf over what the forgivably curious reader/viewer is already having no luck in making out.

Poor Piglet! Had he lived in any part of the Christian era prior to the late nineteenth century, when citizens first began to regard regular household bathing as hygienically imperative rather than weird, his film of valorized ordure would have been considered a sign of healthy good sense. When, for example, it was proposed in 1851 that a complete bathroom be installed in our White House, taxpayers and legislators were outraged by such a frivolous expenditure of public funds. As late as 1906, only one Pittsburgh dwelling in five contained a tub. Yet just twenty years later, as the epistemic ground beneath him begins to crack, Piglet makes himself a butt of humor by trying one last time to adhere to the vanishing paradigm, whose medieval roots are traceable both to *contemptus mundi* and to the misapprehension that dirt provides a shield against the plague. Can the antibacterial sponge and the scented douche be far behind?

We've come a long way, it would appear, from the wholesome sensuality of that sixteenth-century masterpiece *Gargantua*, whose delightfully uninhibited *paidikos phthonos*, or schoolboy malice, stands in melancholy contrast to Christopher Robin's saccharine "goodness." Nowhere in *Pooh*, for example, will we find a counterpart to Rabelais's whole chapter devoted to the multiple and gratifying ways in which the eponymous hero wipes his behind. And when we see young Gargantua sitting in a jakes and fantasizing intercourse with a woman who is simultaneously cleaning her anus with her fingers, we don't immediately think of Milne.

Even so, we know from psychoanalytic research that children today, just like their remote ancestors, "do take delight in their urination, defecation, and vomit."[3] If Pooh lacks not just genitals but also entrails—and therefore both eliminative and digestive functionality—even while he continually eats at a pace that might have wrung a grudging sigh of admiration from Rabelais, the explanation must lie in a volcanic upwelling of sublimation. Luckily for the interests of criticism, however, such censorship is never perfect. The more strenuously an author attempts to efface the body, the more certain it is that telltale signs of the unspeakable will crop up symptomatically in his text.

That return of the repressed is wonderfully dramatized in the memorable episode wherein Pooh, having gorged on honey and condensed milk, gets stuck in the hole that passes for a doorway in Rabbit's burrow. "'Oh, help!' said Pooh. . . . 'Oh, help *and* bother!'" It's important to grasp here that Pooh is completely immobilized, incapable even of jectigation, or jerking of the head. He has become the body

---

3. Alan Hyde, *Bodies of Law* (Princeton: Princeton Univ. Press, 1997), p. 212. Hyde's discussion of "the psychodynamics of urinalysis" (p. 211) can be especially recommended.

as body—for, in Descartes's words, "*le Corps n'est autre chose qu'une statue ou machine de Terre.*" Suspended for indefinite contemplation like a Calderian stabile, Pooh resembles nothing so much as the mummified, museum-bound, aerially dangled *Spirit of St. Louis*, whose famous flight to Paris, with who-knows-what filiations of causal nexus with *Pooh*, would occur just one scant year later.

In the meantime, Pooh is virtually a proctological exhibit protruding into Rabbit's none too capacious dining area. Purportedly scrutinizing an empty can, Rabbit is actually using it as a visual shield to forestall an understandable access of nausea. Yet a whole week will pass before he (and the reader) can be free of this rectal *memento mori*—this vivid and all too cramped juxtaposition of the alimental and the excremental, oppressing the mind with half-conscious thoughts about the decomposition of the condensed milk Pooh has consumed and whence the resultant noxious mess must emerge. Further, the empty honey jar in the dead center of the room portends a debilitating and typically modern sexual revulsion on the part of Rabbit, who has surely been put in mind of the Hamlet who, picturing another room containing an unwelcome extra occupant, reduces one kind of gorging to another when he accuses Gertrude of being "Stewed in corruption, *honeying* and making love / Over a nasty sty."

The sheer domesticity of Rabbit's cozy dwelling is essential to the gruesome effect. We know that the reluctant host will have taken pains to ensure a pleasant room temperature for his own ease and that of his guest's posterior half; yet as we learn from one recent student of the squalid, it is in just such a middling zone of calor that corporeal eruptions of all kinds are most likely to occur: "The boiling and seething of life, the coagulating of blood, the eruption of suppurating sores, the teeming of maggots—disgust itself—operate in what we call the comfort zone."[4]

We will wait in vain, of course, to be shown the bulging, oozing viscera beneath Pooh's hide; nor can modern physiology, with its dry, textbook approach to the body, capture the epic scale and metaphoric richness of their hidden operations. Nonetheless, it seems clear enough that Pooh's predicament is constipation on a truly Rabelaisian scale. The stern-facing Rabbit would be ideally situated to apply a remedy if he happened to have an enema kit in his cupboard. Literalists might say that he is dissuaded simply by concern for the quality of his home environment. It's likelier, however, that having in effect admitted a Trojan bear into his domicile, Rabbit subliminally recalls that the Latin name for Troy, *Ilium*, means precisely the intestinal tract. Either way, there are disincentives to his taking too hasty an approach to reactivating Pooh's colonic contractions.

But what if Pooh, neglected, were to starve to death and begin rotting before he could be removed and safely buried? Here we enter the precinct—namely, putrefaction theory—where Johann Becher (1635–1682) reigned supreme. According to Becher, the miasmas given off by Pooh's decomposing corpse would threaten Rabbit with, at a bare

---

4. William Ian Miller, *The Anatomy of Disgust* (Cambridge: Harvard Univ. Press, 1997), p. 64. The same scholar, by the way, must have been exposed in childhood to this very scene of latent riotousness. How else could he have arrived at his characterization of the disgusting as "the utterly familiar guest who threatens to remain" (p. 89)?

minimum, gangrene, syphilis, and scurvy.[5] In this light, Rabbit's *piano piano* efforts to free the catatonic hulk can be understood as self-interestedly prophylactic.

We mustn't, however, allow the gains we have made in retrieving repressed motivation to blind us to the text's manifest squeamishness. Milne seriously asks us to believe that Pooh, that horizontal Porta Potti, will get slender enough merely by remaining motionless, never emitting so much as a plaintive fart, much less a purgative dump. The drastically censored, Sani-Flushed world of this book is the exact opposite of that celebrated *ammoniapolis*, or vast industrial complex for the processing of urine, of which Clément Joseph Garnier so grandly dreamed in 1844.

I found myself in the capital city of Uganda a few weeks ago, receiving a small prize and helping to inaugurate a humanities institute that had been badly needed there. From outside the walls of the presidential mansion, where some of us had assembled for a ceremonial banquet, the piercing screams of bonobos punctuated the small talk within. In answer to a sociable question of mine, the prime minister's wife related that her daughters had not as yet submitted to clitoridectomy. But the topic led her to forward some interesting news about my own country, divulged by a prior guest. Had I heard, she asked, that a company called Pacer Technology has been seeking government approval of a glue-like product that

---

5. See Alain Corbin, *The Foul and the Fragrant: Odor and the French Social Imagination* (Cambridge: Harvard Univ. Press, 1986), pp. 16–17. For further insight in the same vein, see Dominique Laporte, *History of Shit* (Cambridge: MIT Press, 2000).

is to be used in slaughterhouses to shut off the contaminated rectal cavities of turkeys and chickens?

No, I replied, I hadn't. Inwardly, however, I was not surprised. As I've been underscoring today, *Pooh* is in most respects a work belonging to our own time and culture. What flows within a major text can and must pump itself through the emotional, intellectual, and socioeconomic plumbing of its age. And at the points where that plumbing inevitably fails, an inquiring mind will stand ready to note a pathology in which literary influence and industrial effluence are wondrously, even aesthetically, conjoined. Quite unwittingly, my Kampalese interlocutor had gifted me with one of those small epiphanies that assure a critic he has been following the right scent all along. Just for a moment, then, even the cries of the bonobos sounded to my ears like applause from a company of colleagues who had been shown how everything quite fabulously connects with everything else.

CHAPTER THREE

The Fissured Subtext: Historical Problematics, the Absolute Cause, Transcoded Contradictions, and Late-Capitalist Metanarrative (in Pooh)

CARLA GULAG

Known for her fierce independence and for her belief in bringing social responsibility directly into the classroom, Carla Gulag took her degrees at the University of California at San Diego, Yale University, and the University of California at Los Angeles. Later, on a postdoctoral fellowship in Paris, she seized the rare opportunity of studying with the eminent Louis Althusser at the Ecole Normale Supérieure and serving as a teaching assistant for his famous course, Ideological State Apparatuses 101. But both her dissertation and her first book, *A Skeleton Key to "The Political Unconscious,"* are dedicated to Professor Fredric Jameson, who served as her adviser at all three of her American universities.

Professor Gulag's academic career thus far has been spent at Duke University, where, helping to staff the Program in Literature and co-administering the ever popular Marxism and Society Program, she has lectured and written widely on topics pertaining to Critical Sociology, Critical Anthropology, Critical Legal Studies, and Critical Criticism. It was her influential graduate seminar Junior Postmodern Literary Dialectic, however, that earned her the cross-departmental chair she now holds at Duke as Joe Camel Professor of Child Development.

POWER to the people!

In his invitation to this forum, Professor N. Mack Hobbs urged us to study one another's draft papers and to highlight points of theoretical conflict with our own premises. In my case, there was no need to ask twice: conflict is what Marxist theory is all about. And while every school of criticism these days is concerned to show how it stands to the left of all the others, we Marxists have the advantage of actually being, not just posing as, the authentic radicals.

It's true, I grant, that in a certain broad sense we are all Marxists now. Two years ago, for example, the entire membership of the Modern Language Association ratified the Delegate Assembly's finding that "the capitalist system cannot provide full employment at a living wage" and that MLA'ers therefore have a responsibility "to expose the failures of the current socioeconomic system" at every opportunity. That was one among several encouraging signs that left-wing activism has become the official mission of language and literature teachers. Without a widely obeyed revolutionary vanguard at the helm, however, little has been accomplished beyond the passing of feel-good resolutions.

And when it comes to putting our principles into our literary criticism, there's even less to cheer about.

With or without Hobbs's prompting, I wouldn't have been able to remain silent about the two extraordinary papers that you've all just heard. Neither Felicia Marronnez nor Victor Fassell appears to have overcome the pretheoretical bias that kept literary criticism playing with its weenie in a sandbox for so many decades—the bias, namely, in favor of "explicating the meaning" of one work and even one passage at a time. I find this retrogression especially surprising in the deconstructionist Marronnez. Wasn't it her fellow Derridean Jonathan Culler who established, almost twenty years ago, that despite the many tasks facing criticism, "one thing we do not need is more interpretations of literary works"?[1] Yet here she is, at the start of the third millennium, still hungering after the "significance" of "TRESPASSERS W" and of Pooh's dozing on a rock.

And Fassell—what was his paper called, "Much Nothing about Doo-Doo"? Think of the precious minutes that our ambitious "negotiationist" wasted in attempting to extract salacious and scatalogical implications from visual details in *Winnie-the-Pooh*. If Fassell had read nothing beyond the first sentence of Fredric Jameson's *Signatures of the Visible*, he would have learned that "the visual is *essentially* pornographic."[2] That being so, what could be the point of trying to prove it all over again with examples?

---

1. Jonathan Culler, *The Pursuit of Signs: Semiotics, Literature, Deconstruction* (Ithaca: Cornell Univ. Press, 1981), p. 6.
2. Fredric Jameson, *Signatures of the Visible* (New York and London: Routledge, 1990), p. 1; emphasis in original.

Fassell and Marronnez apparently share the illusion that cited passages from a text "build up a case" for a given reading. Presumably, then, they themselves arrived at their divergent takes on *Winnie-the-Pooh* by open-mindedly "examining the evidence"—a pious fraud that lends an air of neutrality to interpretations that are actually political through and through. And most of you are taken in, because Marronnez's and Fassell's politics—an insistence on academic business as usual while exploited millions suffer and die—strikes you not as reactionary quietism but as professional competence. Meanwhile, the truly essential tasks of criticism—cognitive mapping, reconciling emergent and residual forms, weighing synchronic against diachronic factors, detecting and disabling master narratives, retotalizing the Real, and deciding what is hegemonic over what, and why—remain unaddressed.

I can show you a better model, a fully materialist one, if you will put your false consciousness in abeyance for twenty minutes and really listen. "As a scientific practice," Catherine Belsey has observed, Marxist analysis "is not a process of recognition but work to produce meaning."[3] Produce it, not discover it! Again, Pierre Macherey wisely tells us to "beware of all forms of empiricism, for the objects of any rational investigation have no prior existence."[4] And Fredric Jameson, decisively settling the matter, enjoins us as critics to "liberate [ourselves] from the empirical object."[5] The progressive critic will replace her initial subjective responses with a dialecti-

3. Catherine Belsey, *Critical Practice* (London: Methuen, 1980), p. 138.

4. Pierre Macherey, *A Theory of Literary Production*, trans. Geoffrey Wall (London: Routledge, 1978), p. 5.

5. Fredric Jameson, *The Political Unconscious: Narrative as a Socially Symbolic Act* (Ithaca: Cornell Univ. Press, 1981), p. 297.

cally correct overview that, in Jameson's words, "liquidates the experiences in question and dissolves them without a trace."[6] We aren't fully participating in Marx's tradition until this *liquidation* has occurred.

When a Fassell or a Marronnez tries to explain the gaps and fissures in a literary text by reference to the private authorial mind irrespective of its material determinants, the result is bound to be trifling and erroneous. Lacking awareness that History is the Absolute Cause of absolutely everything, such critics fail to see that every literary work implies the whole foreordained course of social transformation, beginning with the expropriation of surplus labor value by the hereditary gentry, and then by capitalists, and continuing to the final overturning of the "immutable" social order. A critic must—I said she *must*—remain alert at all times to this overarching pattern if she isn't to become a lackey of counterrevolutionary elements.

To see what happens when this mandate is ignored, consider Fassell's lame attempt to determine the meaning of Pooh's weeklong intrusion into Rabbit's quarters. Our New Critic in sunglasses and sandals made a decent start by concentrating on the intestinal stink that's absent from that scene, and he was posing the right question when he asked what is being repressed. But since he won't admit that the individual Freudian unconscious has been irreversibly *transcoded* by Jameson into the Political Unconscious—that is, into History's own instrument for speaking through the author's unsuspecting words—Fassell perceives nothing in the text but an insignificant personal "case."

---

6. Jameson, *Signatures*, p. 4.

A Marxist would have known a priori that the episode points to something more historically consequential than the quote-unquote "timeless" operation of digestive organs that are common to quote-unquote "mankind." The Political Unconscious decided long ago that the ideologeme (Jameson's term) of waste expulsion will always refer to exclusion from the ruling circles. It follows that Milne's squeamishness on the topic boils down to a strictly determined, historically unavoidable inability to come to terms with potentially inflammatory class differences between the possessive home owner Rabbit and the itinerant beggar Pooh.

Knowing how animals traditionally mark their territory, we could say that Pooh, had he pooped on Rabbit's floor, would have established a kind of squatter's right to the premises. That's just the sort of privilege-annihilating development that every progressive could applaud. But the ownership theme can emerge only surreptitiously, in unconscious self-parody, as Rabbit, by hanging his wash on "the South end" of his new doorstop, at once alludes (by denial) to the unspeakable threat of soiling, reasserts his supposed property rights, and reminds us that lands below the equator are those most susceptible to neocolonial exploitation.

Likewise, more is involved in Piglet's dirt rolling than Fassell's universalistic mystifications about reified "nudity and sexual identity." The obsession with filth that took shape in the nineteenth century and carried into the twentieth was essentially a movement against the poor, whose supposedly incurable "bad hygiene" meant that they had to be kept from mingling with their oppressors. By caking himself in dirt, Piglet is reasserting his class identity and thus preserving himself from social castration by the whitening, starching, homogenizing influence of that sylvan soccer mom, Kanga. The soil compacted in his bulletproof vest is nothing less than his brown badge of courage in the industrial army that will eventually beat its plowshares into victorious revolutionary swords.

You can call this just another interpretation if you like, but the point isn't simply to repair the damage wrought by Fassell's bourgeois reading; it's to show you that the text makes no sense at all except in dialectical-materialist terms. Marxism, you see, isn't one item among many that you might sample from the methodological salad bar. It's what Jameson has called "the absolute horizon of all reading and all interpretation," and therefore it's "something like an ultimate *semantic* precondition for the intelligibility of literary and cultural texts."[7] Furthermore, since all non-Marxist critics have repressed that very fact, it follows that Marxism is the only critical idiom that's *not* ideological, or ruled by hidden prejudice. Jameson has said so himself.

In most respects, the workings of the Political Unconscious in *Pooh* are easy enough to decipher. The characters' classless equality and their lack of anything in particular that needs doing indicate that they dwell at either the beginning or the end of History—that is, either before or after the several cycles of exploitation that began with the earliest organized exchange of goods and services. But which period is it? At first glance, the *Pooh* world looks like a good match for that distant Edenic past in which, as Jameson relates, our ancestors experienced such blissful oneness with nature that

7. Jameson, *Political Unconscious*, pp. 17, 75.

they didn't even perceive themselves to be individuals. The point appears to be settled when, in *Postmodernism*, Jameson discloses that early members of our species "bumped into each other a lot, were frequently confused, had short attention spans, and generally milled around aimlessly without identifiable purpose or goals."[8] If that isn't Milne's tribe of dimwits exactly, I don't know what is.

Still, there's a problem here—a problem called Christopher Robin. He is a distinctly superior figure who, however, behaves neither like a feudal lord nor like a robber baron; he just drops in from time to time to see how his little friends are doing and to lend a helping hand when they're confused. What phase of History is this? The answer, I think, can be found in Marx's realization that even after the proletariat's victory, a prolonged transition to the stateless paradise will have to be endured. The backward peasant masses and brutalized industrial laborers, suddenly unoppressed, will need to learn the value of their new condition from a benevolent leader who will gently answer their questions and guide their first halting attempts at self-governance.

In the founding years of the People's Republic of China, Mao Zedong was just such a mild educator. Although we've all been subjected, as Jameson points out, to a "propaganda campaign, everywhere in the world, to Stalinize and discredit Maoism," Mao's doctrine was actually the "richest of all the great new ideologies of the 60s."[9] There

---

8. Fredric Jameson, *Postmodernism, or, The Cultural Logic of Late Capitalism* (Durham: Duke Univ. Press, 1991), p. 218.
9. Fredric Jameson, *The Ideologies of Theory: Essays, 1971–1986*, vol. 2: *The Syntax of History* (Minneapolis: Univ. of Minnesota Press, 1988), pp. 189, 188.

was violence in the thriving young democracy, to be sure; but since "violence springs from counterrevolution first and foremost,"[10] we can't blame it on Mao, whose only mistake was to rein in the Red Guards before they could enact what Jameson had hoped would be "the ultimate consequences" of the Cultural Revolution.[11] In that show of softheartedness, Mao displayed the same peaceable avuncularity as Christopher Robin, whom we can now correctly identify, in the Political Unconscious of *Pooh*, as a proleptic Mao figure.

We Marxist intellectuals have our own Mao, of course, a secular fisher of men who happens to have written the "*summa marxologica* for our time."[12] Could he, too, be prefigured in Christopher Robin? Although certain "historical conditions of possibility . . . set the stage for the discursive subject 'Fredric Jameson' to be the bearer of a *possible* ideological project," James Kavanagh has remarked, "this project was so effectively realized only because a lived subject (however fictional and precarious) made a disciplined, comprehensive, and immanent appropriation-critique of virtually every critical language issuing from the crevices of the Western

---

10. Jameson, *Postmodernism*, p. 402.

11. Jameson, *Syntax of History*, pp. 207–8. Even well after the Cultural Revolution, Julia Kristeva still found Mao's soothing influence everywhere, as she reported after a three-week visit: "The so-called sexual relations do not seem to be centered on transgression: the quest for partial objects, perversions, etc. A genitality—that is, a passage through the oedipal stage— . . . seems to rule this scene and imparts a relaxed, calm, 'maternal' atmosphere to the street, to the workplace, even to holidays such as May 1." Julia Kristeva, *Polylogues* (Paris: Editions du Seuil, 1977), p. 522.

12. Dominick LaCapra, review of *The Political Unconscious*, by Fredric Jameson, *History and Theory* 21 (1982), p. 83.

ideological apparatus."[13] In this one instance it seems possible that the Dialectic suspended its usual tortuous course and intervened directly in human affairs.

I hazard this hypothesis because Jameson walks the earth at a moment when his wise counsel is desperately needed. It is a time, frankly, when further disputation over *Winnie-the-Pooh* looks to be a luxury we can ill afford. All around us on the left, for example, we see signs of premature antifascism, even though we know perfectly well that the capitalist order must be allowed to pass through a fascist stage before its ultimate collapse. Yet if we could only school ourselves to follow in Jameson's patient footsteps, we could be sure of treading the historically sanctioned path.

Thus, in the face of hysterical ranting over the Paul de Man flap, Jameson has serenely observed that de Man's service to *Le Soir* in the forties, when his Nazi employers (like all employers) required his product to meet certain expectations, was "simply a job."[14] In fact, it was scarcely different from A. A. Milne's job of writing light verse for the imperialist magazine *Punch*. To be sure, de Man was then rationalizing the Wehrmacht's occupation of his native Belgium. But that's what History wanted the Third Reich to be doing just then, and somebody else would have shown the required hospitality if de Man hadn't pitched in. Moreover, Jameson has shown, neither then nor later did de Man stoop to the really serious vulgarity of expressing anti-Communist sentiments. And surely he was no worse than Martin Heidegger,

13. James Kavanagh, "The Jameson-Effect," *New Orleans Review* 11 (1984), p. 20.

14. Jameson, *Postmodernism*, p. 257.

whose straightforward "political commitment" to Hitler, Jameson has noted, was "morally and aesthetically preferable to apolitical liberalism."[15]

Today, under Late Capitalism, it is more essential than ever to heed Jameson's warning that the system still has some ripening to do before it falls. When Lenin wrote about Late Capitalism, he had in mind an imperialist Monopoly Stage that would be the final one. As Jameson remarks, however, "late" now "rarely means anything so silly as the ultimate senescence, breakdown, and death of the system as such. . . . What 'late' generally conveys is rather the sense that something has changed, that things are different."[16] My own guess is that Late Capitalism is "late"—quite a bit behind schedule—for an appointment with its own demise. Thus, to the known sins of this despicable regime must be added still another, procrastination.

If, under Late Capitalism, culture itself ceases to be a site of resistance and becomes integrated into a worldwide hyperspatial "culture industry" of simulacra manipulated by giants of oligopoly more powerful than any Repressive State Apparatus; if "the prodigious new expansion of multinational capital ends up penetrating and colonizing those very precapitalist enclaves (Nature and the Unconscious) which offered . . . footholds for critical effectivity";[17] if the whole

---

15. Jameson, *Postmodernism*, p. 257. Heidegger's enthusiasm eventually abated, but for a good ideological reason. Along with members of "the revolutionary (anticapitalist) left within National Socialism," he finally became disillusioned, understandably, with "Hitler's pragmatic position as a moderate or centrist" (*Postmodernism*, p. 257).

16. Jameson, *Postmodernism*, p. xxi.

17. Jameson, *Postmodernism*, p. 49.

planet is becoming one vast standardized corporate theme park from which "reality" has been tidied out of sight—then we can only steel ourselves to wait, as Jameson advises, for the inevitable emergence of a new international proletariat that will be markedly more unified and militant than the last.[18]

This *will* happen, of course: it is History's plan. As Enrique Dussel points out in a book co-edited by Jameson, "The globalizing world-system reaches a limit with the exteriority of the alterity of the Other, a locus of 'resistance' from whose affirmation the process of the negation of negation of liberation begins."[19] Thus we must regard Late Capitalism and its cultural offspring, postmodernism, as positive and necessary mutations of the Monopoly Stage. But if so, there is an important corollary to be taken to heart by Marxist cultural workers here and now. We need to stop resisting postmodern corporatism and its packaged pleasures—no, better, we need to help them along, secure in our knowledge that we are thereby greasing History's rails.

As you might expect, once again Fred Jameson can be found far ahead of the curve. It is time, he shows, for Marxists to climb down from their rickety barricades and cultivate "a specific enjoyment of the potentialities of the material body."[20] Look at the progress he himself has already made:

---

18. See Jameson, *Syntax of History*, p. 208.

19. Enrique Dussel, "Beyond Eurocentrism: The World-System and the Limits of Modernity," in *The Cultures of Globalization*, ed. Fredric Jameson and Masao Miyoshi (Durham and London: Duke Univ. Press, 1998), p. 21.

20. Jameson, *Syntax of History*, p. 74.

I write as a relatively enthusiastic consumer of post-modernism . . . : I like the architecture and a lot of the newer visual work, in particular the newer photography. The music is not bad to listen to, or the poetry to read; . . . subgeneric narratives [of the novel] are very good, indeed. . . . Food and fashion have also greatly improved, as has the life world generally.[21]

As this last sentence implies, it's not enough to indulge our eyes and ears; we should also be out there on the front lines buying postmodern merchandise. So much the better if it has been produced by alienated multinational labor, sub-subsistence wages, denuded tropical forests, mergered corporatist cunning, offshore laundered finance, and cross-border ruses of hedged arbitrage and import-duty evasion. All of those practices must gain momentum in preparation for the coming proletarian explosion. Instead of sitting around reading a tame modernist text like *Pooh*, then, a good postmodern Marxist might want to log on to the Toys "Я" Us Web site and order a vertically integrated Disney knockoff such as a My Interactive Pooh™ or a Bounce Around Tigger.™

The only stipulation that Fred places on Late Capitalist pleasures is that they be "allegorical"—that is, "able to stand as a figure for the transformation of social relations as a whole."[22] His classic example—set forth in *Postmodernism*, the book that won the MLA's 1991 James Russell Lowell Prize for "outstanding literary or linguistic study"—is the delight

---

21. Jameson, *Postmodernism*, pp. 298–99.
22. Jameson, *Syntax of History*, p. 73.

that can be had on the elevators and escalators of a postmodern hotel like the Westin Bonaventure in Los Angeles.

Even a hotel, Fred discovered, can harbor a teasing Political Unconscious that invites us to loosen up and live a little. It had never previously come to my notice that elevators and escalators, those "dialectical opposites," as Fred says, zip us back and forth so "breathtakingly and even alarmingly" that we can't even find the interior boutiques.[23] That's why—and here comes the allegorical part—"the commercial tenants are in despair and all the merchandise is marked down to bargain prices."[24] Surely that is a foretaste of the coming worldwide crash that will be so gratifying. I propose that you yourselves, instead of rushing off this afternoon to the Madonna Studies No-Host Cash Bar, try some allegorical escalating and elevating right here in the Washington Hilton.

The Revolution expects no less of you. ¡*Venceremos!*

---

23. Jameson, *Postmodernism*, pp. 43–44.
24. Jameson, *Postmodernism*, p. 44.

CHAPTER FOUR

Just Lack a Woman

SISERA CATHETER

Since her undergraduate years, when she led a successful movement to keep her women's college uncorrupted by male admissions, Sisera Catheter's uppermost concern has been gender justice. Later, as a young faculty leader at Kenyon College, she spearheaded that institution's proactively feminist reform of its curriculum, hiring and promotion standards, pronoun vigilance, and permission-to-proceed agreements for cross-gender physical contact. And more recently, as director of Women's Studies at the University of Massachusetts, she helped to draft *Vision 2000*, a policy document aiming to ensure, among other goals, that nonfeminist faculty members in the six New England land-grant universities be excluded from consideration for merit raises.*

---

*See New England Council of Land-Grant University Women, *Vision 2000* (1997), http://www.umass.edu/wost/articles/vision2K/whole.htm.

Professor Catheter is best known, however, for her avidly studied publications, which trenchantly combine activist militancy and theoretical rigor. They include *Stormin' Normativity*, *I Sing the Body Eclectic*, *Theory of Corporeality / Corporeality of Theory*, and *The Purr-Loined Let-Her*. Of particular relevance to this present volume are Catheter's two book-length contributions to criticism of children's literature, *Deviance, Defiance, Mary Poppins* and *Moonlight Dentata: What Sendak Fears*. As the editor of the fanzine *Sissy Rules!* has written of her, "It's Sissy or nobody, baby, if you want to kick ass and devalorize the heteropatriarchy's sham territoriality."

The Feminine is the silent Phallic Mother who is always already lost in castration. But she is also the freedom of not being bound by the law of castration which has not yet been achieved.

—Jeanne Lorraine Schroeder

What has she got in that firm little fist of hers?
Somebody's thumb, and it feels like Christopher's.
—A. A. Milne

SUPPOSE we get a few things straight before some members of this very mixed audience begin to form sentimental misconceptions. First, I haven't come all this way to exchange "insights" with literary hobbyists and brat huggers. Gynocritical discourse isn't just a "school of criticism" like any other. It partakes of a much wider project: the rescue of Earth itself from the gender that has brought it to the brink of catastrophe. From that rape manual of soulless science, Newton's *Principia*, through the testosterone-fueled equation $E=mc^2$, phallocognition has saddled us with a predatory and potentially suicidal antagonism to nature.[1] That horror is what prompted Mary Daly—who was forced into retirement from Boston College by priests and phallocrats just because she had the good sense to exclude males from her classes—to declare, "Phallic myth and language generate, legitimate, and mask the material pollution that threatens to terminate all sentient life on this planet."[2]

As long as I've got control of this microphone, then, we're going to be in emergency mode. Obviously, we'll want to avoid clinically "objective" masculinist analysis—the literary-critical equivalent of the sadistic gynecological workup.[3] As Daly has said, "Since the 'unknown' is stolen/ hidden know-ing, frozen and stored by the Abominable Snowmen of Androcratic Academia, Spinsters must melt these masses of 'knowledge' with the fire of female fury."[4]

---

1. It was Sandra Harding who brought Newton's molestational intent to light. See Harding, *The Science Question in Feminism* (Ithaca: Cornell Univ. Press, 1986), p. 113. And Luce Irigaray gets the credit for having challenged Einstein's overrated equation, which "privileges the speed of light over other speeds that are vitally necessary to us." Irigaray, "Sujet de la science, sujet sexué?" in *Sens et place des connaissances dans la société, 3ᵉ confrontation*, ed. Action Locale Bellevue (Paris: Centre National de Recherche Scientifique, 1987), p. 110.

2. Mary Daly, *Gyn/Ecology* (Boston: Beacon Press, 1978), p. 9.

3. For vivid discussions of pelvic prying, see Terri Kapsalis, *Public Privates: Performing Gynecology from Both Ends of the Speculum* (Durham and London: Duke Univ. Press, 1997), and Katharine Young, *Presence in the Flesh: The Body in Medicine* (Cambridge: Harvard Univ. Press, 1998). Under examination, a woman's body gets "reconstituted in different universes of discourse," observes Young. "Dismantling the body into its discourses does not dematerialize the body but rather has its footing in embodiment" (pp. 78–79). And that hurts!

4. Daly, *Gyn/Ecology*, p. 8.

Do I detect a dissenting smirk on certain hirsute faces? If so, a small reminder may be timely. Almost a decade ago, the MLA's Committee on the Status of Women in the Profession identified "antifeminist harassment" as a grave and growing menace. Not harassment of *women*, which is bad enough, but intolerable disrespect toward *feminism*, including such offenses as "malicious humor" and the deprecation of feminist work as "narrow," "partisan," or "lacking in rigor." Need I point out that we're attending an MLA meeting today? If anyone thinks that feminism is narrow, partisan, or funny, just stand up and let all of us know who you are.[5]

No takers? In that case, let's make sure that our feminism itself is sufficiently ready for battle with the offensively boy-ish text before us. Twenty or thirty years ago, our elder sis-ters thought they would be fulfilling their mission if they merely brought to light "the representation of woman" in one male "classic" after another. In *Pooh*'s case, they would have been satisfied to show how two "feminine" figures, Kanga and Daphne Milne—one peripherally included in the story, the other quarantined within its fulsome dedication, "To Her . . . Because We Love You"—purportedly exert a softening "motherly influence" on the whole. Such a femi-nism, we now recognize, had its own perversely maternal

---

5. Needless to say, this challenge was not addressed to male feminists, who, as Sandra Harding points out, can "advance the understandings produced by women feminists. They can teach and write about women's thought, writ-ings, accomplishments. . . . They can criticize their male colleagues. They can move material resources to women and feminists." Sandra Harding, "Who Knows? Identities and Feminist Epistemology," in *Engendering Knowl-edge*, ed. Joan E. Hartman and Ellen Messer-Davidow (Knoxville: Univ. of Tennessee Press, 1991), p. 109.

role to play, that of rescuing books like Milne's from condemnation as the blatantly sexist performances that they are.

Daphne, the ideal mother? Why do you suppose Milne senior found himself monopolizing his little son's story time? "Daphne was glad enough to have [Christopher Robin] safely away at boarding school for weeks at a time," writes the family biographer, "—and rarely went near the school."[6] Her marriage was a total bust. That's why she took to sailing across the Atlantic on a regular basis to get it on with the American playwright Elmer Rice.[7] And why not, since her celebrated mate had already begun his own dalliance with the actress Leonora Corbett? The dedication of *Pooh* was a feeble cover-up that didn't fool anyone who knew what the Milne household was really like.

As for Kanga, if you think she embodies a genuine tribute to Woman, what do you make of this line from an early draft of the book: "Every Tuesday Kanga spent the day with *his* great friend Pooh"?[8] When Milne finally consented to make "him" female, the accompanying plot element was foreordained: a scheme to expel "her" from the bachelor pad Forest once and for all. You can actually see, from a Shepard illustration, Pooh's alarm at the moment he spots Kanga's "pouch" and realizes that his "great friend" is no longer one of the gang. It's a scene straight out of *Boys Don't Cry*.

---

6. Ann Thwaite, *A. A. Milne: The Man behind Winnie-the-Pooh* (New York: Random House, 1990), p. 388.
7. See Ann Thwaite, *The Brilliant Career of Winnie-the-Pooh: The Definitive History of the Best Bear in All the World* (New York: Dutton Children's Books, 1994), p. 137.
8. Thwaite, *Brilliant Career*, p. 85; emphasis added.

The text as we have it, of course, does portray Kanga as "the mother"—specifically, as a close-binding-intimate one who hovers over her hyperactive, accident-prone son, Roo, while continually nagging and bossing him. Her "humorous" byplay with the baby-kangaroo imposter Piglet, by parodying this overprotectiveness, only serves to emphasize it. We can easily infer, then, why the half-suffocated Roo behaves in such a desperately manic, exhibitionistic way. "Look at me swimming! . . . Did you see me swimming?" We saw you, kid; and we foresee therapy for you.

Every male infant's aim, we learn from Melanie Klein, "is to possess himself of the contents of the mother's body and to destroy her by means of every weapon which sadism can command."[9] A smother-mother like Kanga, snuffing out that healthy desire before it can properly take hold, hurries her son along prematurely to the next stage of pseudomasculine identity formation, in which he "exchanges something he does not have (access to the Phallic Mother, identity with the Feminine) for something that does not exist (the *Phallus*, access to the Feminine) in order to achieve something with no content (subjectivity)."[10] No wonder the little jumping jack expends so much energy asserting a selfhood that is actually null and void.

I must admit that the misogynist Milne has done a deft job of depicting Kanga as the quintessential female airhead.

---

9. Melanie Klein, *Love, Guilt, and Reparation and Other Works* (London: Hogarth Press, 1975), p. 219.
10. Jeanne Lorraine Schroeder, *The Vestal and the Fasces: Hegel, Lacan, Property, and the Feminine* (Berkeley, Los Angeles, and London: Univ. of California Press, 1998), p. 85.

Her speech never wavers from the blandest and most cloying "motherese," and we think we'll retch if she says "Now, Roo, dear" one more time. But the great Parisian feminists of the seventies and eighties—above all, Luce Irigaray, Julia Kristeva, and Hélène Cixous—have taught us how to stand such a demeaning portrait on its head. Kanga is indeed Woman, but Woman as she has been abjected by centuries of forced acculturation to the sick gynophobic demands of the patriarchy. And in that light she can be seen by us, if not by Milne, as a virtual poster girl for the struggle against male oppression.

Kanga fits perfectly, for example, with the French feminists' unanimous conclusion that "all women are neurotic" and have been so for "thousands of years";[11] that up till now our whole gender has shown itself to be "temperamental, incomprehensible, perturbed, capricious";[12] and that we've been out of sync with linear chronological time, incapable of handling money or property, and maladapted to any investigation of male-defined "reality."[13] These are hard lessons to absorb, but once we and Kanga have accepted them, men can't do any further damage to our self-respect.

A male chauvinist, for example, couldn't very well charge Kanga with sounding silly and stupid if she'd already reached the same conclusion herself. As Irigaray observes, there's more than a hint of senile dementia in our normal

11. Marguerite Duras, in *New French Feminisms: An Anthology*, ed. Elaine Marks and Isabelle de Courtivron (New York: Schocken, 1981), p. 176.

12. Luce Irigaray, *Ce sexe qui n'en est pas un* (Paris: Minuit, 1977), p. 28.

13. See the discussion of Julia Kristeva in Toril Moi, *Sexual/Textual Politics: Feminist Literary Theory* (London and New York: Routledge, 1985), p. 114; Irigaray, *Ce sexe*, p. 30; and Hélène Cixous, "Castration or Decapitation?" trans. Annette Kuhn, *Signs* 7, no. 1 (1981), p. 45.

social utterance; and our efforts at mature symbolic construction can only render us, in Kristeva's bitter assessment, "ecstatic, nostalgic, or mad."[14] Living under the merciless gaze of the enemy, we find that our options come down to either chirpily mimicking the master discourse, as Milne forces Kanga to do, or producing what Toril Moi, paraphrasing Irigaray, calls Woman's "incomprehensible babble."[15]

But what would be the speech quality of a fully liberated Kanga? Once again, French feminism has already supplied the answer: a "discourse of the clitoris in the mucus of the lips."[16] Because our labia are pressed together nearly all the time, you see, we females move about in a state of perpetual masturbation. Hence our natural, uninhibited language, being "determined by the friction between two infinitely neighboring forces," ought to be "continuous, compressible, dilatable, viscous, conductive, diffusible."[17] And that's what Kanga would sound like if she didn't have to serve as Milne's marionette mom.

But with whom, in the *Pooh* world, could a sexually and politically aroused Kanga speak? So long as she has to keep prostituting herself to Roo's father, who seems to have returned home from his philandering just long enough to knock her up, there's no hope for her emancipation. And meanwhile, she finds herself trapped in an "enchanted forest"—no, make that a Bohemian Grove—ruled by a cabal of

---

14. See Moi, *Sexual/Textual Politics*, p. 127; and Julia Kristeva, *The Kristeva Reader*, ed. Toril Moi (Oxford: Blackwell, 1986), p. 150.

15. Moi, *Sexual/Textual Politics*, p. 135.

16. Gayatri Chakravorty Spivak (characterizing Irigaray's idea), in *Outside in the Teaching Machine* (New York and London: Routledge, 1993), p. 170.

17. Irigaray, *Ce sexe*, pp. 109–10.

self-satisfied studs. What's the use, then, of our marching around with placards reading FREE THE MARSUPIAL ONE? Kanga is stuck, and we ourselves are stuck with a disgusting stag-party *Pooh*.

We've reached a crisis point now, one that every feminist critic will find all too familiar. At a certain moment the demon voice of the patriarchy always whispers insinuatingly in our ear, "Honey, this just isn't your kind of book. Give it up, why don't you?" But we can't get disheartened just because the only female character in *Pooh* is marginalized and adulterated. Remember, radical feminism never aims at a positivistic mirroring of the author's intentions. As Sandra Harding puts it, "Feminist claims should be held not as 'approximations to truth' but as permanently partial instigators of rupture, of rents and unravelings in the dominant schemes of representation."[18] Since those rents are already "there" in the precarious construction of masculinity, they ought to be discernible behind the façade of heartiness in masculine prose. There's hope, then, that some well-aimed kicks can produce a nice big rupture in Milne's testicular textuality.

For starters, let me call your attention to a feature of *Pooh* that even the most reactionary reader would have to recognize as "really there"—an obsessive insecurity about selfhood:

"Hallo, Rabbit, isn't that you?"

"No," said Rabbit, in a different sort of voice this time.

---

18. Sandra Harding, "Feminist Justificatory Strategies," in *Women, Knowledge, and Reality: Explorations in Feminist Philosophy*, ed. Ann Garry and Marilyn Pearsall (Boston: Unwin Hyman, 1989), p. 198.

"But isn't that Rabbit's voice?"

"I don't *think* so," said Rabbit. "It isn't *meant* to be."

"I am *not* Roo," said Piglet loudly. "I am Piglet!" . . .

"If you go on making faces like Piglet's, you will grow up to *look* like Piglet—and *then* think how sorry you will be."

"Hallo!" said Tigger. "I've found somebody just like me. I thought I was the only one of them."

"It's Eeyore!" cried Roo, terribly excited.

"Is that so?" said Eeyore . . . "I wondered."

Note that it's only the male characters—and *all* of the male characters—who are made uneasy about their identity. They are, shall we say, less than cocksure as to who they are. There seems to be a certain estrangement between the *Pooh* males' executive ego upstairs and the reluctant John Henry who's supposed to be doing the heavy lifting below. And in this respect they're just like men in general, who are never free from anxiety about the inflatability-on-command of what Cixous once called their "little pocket signifier."

True enough, "possession of a penis . . . gives men a direct bodily relation to the phallus."[19] Yet Jacques Lacan, in a virtuoso exercise of non-Euclidean math, famously assessed

---

19. Susan Sellers, *Language and Sexual Difference: Feminist Writing in France* (New York: St. Martin's, 1991), p. 84. Sellers here reports a discovery made by the French psychoanalyst / feminist Eugénie Lemoine-Luccioni.

that phallus as merely the square root of minus 1.[20] Nor is that the worst of it. The phallus, Judith Butler has shown, is just a marker for desire, and desire itself is only "that which guarantees a certain opacity in language."[21] Try waving *that* around, fellows!

Even so retrograde a commentator as Victor Fassell has told us, in his typically waffling way, that the *Pooh* animals may possibly be hermaphrodites. If so, they would be no more unusual than the dachshund in Munro Leaf's *Noodle*, a children's book that plainly expresses "a wish to have both male and female genitalia."[22] But hermaphroditism would be a pleasant dilemma compared to the psychological devastation we can make out below the bland surface of *Pooh*.

"There is a hole, a lie, and a fiction at the heart of subjectivity"[23]—well, of male subjectivity, anyway. It displays itself most starkly when, in chapter 4 of *Winnie-the-Pooh*, Pooh and Eeyore lose their composure upon discovering the absence of Eeyore's tail:

> So Eeyore stood there, gazing sadly at the ground, and Winnie-the-Pooh walked all round him once.
>
> "Why, what's happened to your tail?" he said in surprise.

20. Jacques Lacan, *Ecrits: A Selection*, trans. Alan Sheridan (New York and London: Norton, 1977), pp. 317–20.

21. Judith Butler, "Desire," in *Critical Terms for Literary Study*, 2nd ed., ed. Frank Lentricchia and Thomas McLaughlin (Chicago and London: Univ. of Chicago Press, 1995), p. 369.

22. Ellen Handler Spitz, *Inside Picture Books* (New Haven and London: Yale Univ. Press, 1999), p. 173.

23. Schroeder, *Vestal*, pp. 86–87.

"What *has* happened to it?" said Eeyore.

"It isn't there!"

"Are you sure?"

"Well, either a tail *is* there or it isn't there. You can't make a mistake about it. And yours *isn't* there!"

"Then what is?"

"Nothing."

Seeing himself castrated and thus ineluctably "female," Eeyore bends his head between and behind his forepaws, evidently attempting an acrobatic autoerotic feat that, if successful, will not only restore his depleted narcissistic libido and give him something to chew on that's nicer than thistles but also exchange his former adult self for a polymorphous perversity whereby the oral, anal, and genital stages can merge in an endless preoedipal, nonphallic loop. In short, he is so unsure of his maleness that he now hopes to transform himself into an unborn baby woman.

The Shepard illustration showing Pooh's initial reaction to the missing tail is no less psychologically revealing. By reflexively inserting one paw in his mouth, Pooh enviously acknowledges the unconscious significance of Eeyore's maneuver. With his other paw he nervously checks his crotch, which offers no more reassurance of phallicity than he has gleaned from his voyeuristic, but also distinctly priapic, gazing at Eeyore's rear end. In this split second when Eeyore appears most invitingly available to be sodomized, the abashed Pooh realizes that the requisite tool is missing. If "Woman as lack is constitutive of gendered subjectivity,"[24] the unasked-for *pres-*

---

24. Schroeder, *Vestal*, p. 61n.

ence of that lack in every pixel of the unconsummated rape tableau hurls gendered subjectivity right out the window.[25]

The demasculinized Eeyore seems to be on the verge of comprehending, in the words of Judith Butler quoting Monique Wittig quoting Deleuze and Guattari, that there are "as many sexes as there are individuals."[26] If "there is no possible outline of the body as such," and if bodies "emerge from a discursive project" in the first place, then "the belief that 'one is a woman' is almost as absurd and obscurantist as the belief that 'one is a man.'"[27] When this realization becomes common knowledge, who can say how radically our world will be transformed?

We're making some progress now toward rupturing *Pooh*, but gender uncertainty per se is too private a matter to get the whole job done. Nor can we do much damage by pointing out that the *Pooh* males are all fetishists in search of substitute penises. Most readers perversely think that fetishism is just plain cute:

---

25. How many genitals are missing when Pooh and Eeyore have finished playing doctor? According to the phallomorphic logic of old-time feminism, the answer is of course two, or one putz per animal. In a magisterial intervention, however, Jane Gallop has argued that each not-yet-castrated male possesses *three* sex organs—the complete pathetic teakettle. Thus the net transfer in this scene of metamorphosis would be minus-six giblets. See Jane Gallop, "Quand nos lèvres s'écrivent: Irigaray's Body Politic," *Romantic Review* 74, no. 1 (1983), pp. 77–83.

26. Judith Butler, *Gender Trouble: Feminism and the Subversion of Identity* (New York and London: Routledge, 1990), p. 118.

27. Here I quote Gayatri Chakravorty Spivak, "In a Word: Interview" [with Ellen Rooney], *differences* 1, no. 2 (1989), p. 148; Donna Haraway, "The Promises of Monsters: A Regenerative Politics for Inappropriate/d Others," in *Cultural Studies*, ed. Lawrence Grossberg, Cary Nelson, and Paula A. Treichler (New York and London: Routledge, 1992), p. 298; and Julia Kristeva, in *New French Feminisms*, ed. Marks and Courtivron, p. 137.

But Piglet wasn't listening, he was so agog at the thought of seeing Christopher Robin's blue braces again. He had only seen them once before, when he was much younger, and, being a little over-excited by them, had had to go to bed half an hour earlier than usual.

In men, though, gender uncertainty usually leads to experimentation with same-sex sex. Though nothing could be more English than that, nothing is considered more threatening to the society at large or to an overcompensating male ego such as Milne's. How telling it is, then, that *Pooh*'s two leading characters enter quite explicitly into a lasting domestic partnership:

> "What would *you* do, if *your* house was blown down?" . . .
>   "He'd come and live with me," said Pooh, "wouldn't you, Piglet?"
>   Piglet squeezed his paw.
>   "Thank you, Pooh," he said. "I should love to."

It's encouraging that the interdigitating *amici* can pull off this gay marriage under the noses not only of the uptight British public but of A. A. Milne himself. Even so, some of us are less than thrilled by the backhanded tribute that gay marriage pays to the most pernicious of all institutions, straight matrimony. And, interestingly enough, the text seems to have its own misgivings on this point. Note, for example, how tame Pooh and Piglet's union looks when juxtaposed with Tigger and Roo's bareback fling in a treetop.

"Pooh, isn't it fun," exclaims Roo, "Tigger and I are living in a tree, like Owl, and we're going to stay here for ever and ever." They don't, of course. Minutes later, Roo gets down to basics: "'Can Tiggers do it?' And he squeaked out: 'I'm coming, Christopher Robin!'" Pooh himself, by the way, seems to decide at a certain point that vows of monogamy with Piglet aren't binding after all. Without so much as blushing, he sings out merrily that "a Help-yourself with Rabbit" is, for him, "a *pleasant* sort of habit."

As for Rabbit, you wouldn't at first think of him in bathhouse terms, because he's the most absurdly "masculine" (gruff, managerial, legalistic, jealousy-ridden) of Milne's characters. But the text can't lie. Sexually inhibited with most of the adults he must dominate, Rabbit vents his dammed-up libido on a boychild: "Rabbit was playing with Baby Roo in his own house, and feeling more fond of him every minute."

Moreover, even Rabbit's paranoid jealousies point to currents of eroticism that have gone unremarked by *Pooh* critics. Eve Kosofsky Sedgwick, who shares my interest in queering masculinist fictions, has shown that male rivalry must always be reconfigured in sexual terms: to want the rival removed is to want the rival, period.[28] In this light, Rabbit turns out to be quite the humping bunny after all. The Sedgwick syndrome explains why he goes to such lengths to "lose"—that is, to strand in the fog—the attractive newcomer Tigger, whose provocative tattoos and pneumatic thrusts have already

---

28. See Eve Kosofsky Sedgwick, *Between Men: English Literature and Male Homosocial Desire*, rev. ed. (New York: Columbia Univ. Press, 1992).

induced Baby Roo's first involuntary ejaculation: "'Oo, Tigger—oo, Tigger—oo, Tigger!' squeaked Roo excitedly."

The episode between Tigger and Rabbit turns horny when the latter realizes that his persecutory compulsion was only a last-ditch effort to stifle his lust for the muscular exotic beast:

> Tigger was tearing round the Forest making loud yapping noises for Rabbit. . . . And the Small and Sorry Rabbit rushed through the mist at the noise, and it suddenly turned into Tigger; a Friendly Tigger, a Grand Tigger, a Large and Helpful Tigger, a Tigger who bounced . . . in just the beautiful way a Tigger ought to bounce.
>
>   "Oh, Tigger, I *am* glad to see you," cried Rabbit.

It would be hard to say which element is most expressive in the accompanying illustration—Rabbit's lascivious leer, the two standing tails, or the displaced pubic hairs that have achieved erections of their own on the tips of the two aroused noses.

Even Eeyore, once his own "tail" has been reattached, appears to have joined the Fire Island–style fireworks in his characteristic downbeat manner. His renowned *tristesse*, so mystifying to superficial critics, is plainly postcoital—indeed postorgiastic. Damage to the overstressed member is his nagging concern:

> "As I expected," he said. "Lost all feeling. Numbed it. That's what it's done. Numbed it. . . ."
>
>   "Poor old Eeyore. I'll dry it for you," said Christopher Robin, . . . rubbing his hardest. "Is *that* better?"
>
>   ". . . It Belongs again, if you know what I mean."

So what's the upshot here—that *Winnie-the-Pooh* is "better literature" than I once thought, or that gay promiscuity is all a radical feminist could ask from a text? Wrong, and wrong again. All I've done is to show you that we don't have to take Milne's sexism lying down on our backs. Any nominally straight text would yield comparable "findings" if we met it with the right kind of resistance.

Even so, I couldn't have made my subversive reading stick without the help of genuine, universal male insecurity, which always shows up wherever you look for it. And this is good news, because "the bi-textuality of the unconscious . . . .threatens the heterosocial control of the Symbolic order."[29] *Pooh* looks ahead, despite its best contrary intentions, to an eventual dismantling of the patriarchy. Until then, boys, I don't care which orifice you choose for sharpening your little pencils; they'll just be useless stubs when *écriture féminine* becomes the official idiom of power.

---

29. Robert Samuels, *Hitchcock's Bi-Textuality: Lacan, Feminisms, and Queer Theory* (Albany: State Univ. of New York Press, 1998), p. 136.

CHAPTER FIVE

The Importance of Being Portly

ORPHEUS BRUNO

The contributor to this volume who is best known to the general public is Orpheus Bruno, Harvard University's Hasty Pudding Theatricals Professor of World Literature. Although his remarkably varied career was well under way when the first anthology of *Pooh* studies appeared in 1963, many more years elapsed before he turned his attention to children's literature. Bruno's early prominence rested chiefly on his critical reassessment of British Romanticism, typified in his iconic study of the Aeolian harp theme, *The Breaking of the Wind* (1962).

In the 1970s, Professor Bruno began turning out books with a frequency rivaling that of Isaac Asimov. And rivalry was precisely his theme. Taking major British poets as his subject matter, Bruno set forth a sweeping theory of creativity based on the novice's need to get out from under his grandest predecessors. Many older scholars still recall the excitement generated by *Writing Is Backbiting* (1971), *Mud Wrestling in the Pantheon* (1973), and *The Savage Sublime: One-Upmanship at the Muses' Gate* (1976).

After a brief foray into biblical studies—notably in *Couching Towards Bethlehem: The Repressed Meaning of the Fourth Synoptic Gospel* (1985)—Professor Bruno began counseling the literate public on cultural matters. His best-known titles in this vein are *My Vico, My Shakespeare, My God!* (1991), *What You Don't Know Hurts Me* (1995), and *Just Read These Books* (1998). Asked about advances that are reputed to reach the high six figures, Bruno invariably quotes Wallace Stevens: "Money is a form of poetry." He is hard at work on his next two volumes, *Bruno Predicts* and *As I Said Before*.

WHAT a strange experience it is to attend a Modern Language convention after staying away for twenty-five years! Scanning your youthfully inexpressive faces, my dears, and thinking back to the days when whole panels were devoted to parsing my work, I am put in mind of Rip Van Winkle returning to his village after having slept through the American Revolution. Of course, I know all about *your* literary-critical revolution—or should I say, with Jimmy Durante, your revoltin' development. Even so, I feel less like an adversary than like a sheer stranger as I swim against the swirling human current in these corridors and visit assorted meeting rooms just long enough to ascertain that no panelist speaks for me, or even to me. How alien the MLA frenzy seems—the desperate, self-important, theory-infatuated scramble to reach the top of an academic anthill.

It's just an expression of the national disorder that D. H. Lawrence captured in the formula *Produce! produce! produce! Destroy! destroy! destroy!*

I'm afraid you're unaware of a vastly different country out there—a spiritually yearning and eternally restless one that pays no heed to the academic rat race. Old infidel Bruno knows, if you don't, that the quintessential Americans aren't Franklin, Edison, and Ford, much less Jameson, Marronnez, and Fassell, but Joseph Smith, Elizabeth Clare Prophet, and David Koresh. More native than Microsoft is the Raëlian religion, which holds that humankind was fashioned in the image of space aliens. Bruno listens with sympathy, if not exactly with agreement, gathering all that metaphysical frenzy into his ample bosom with Whitmanesque inclusiveness. And though he is convinced that the Creation was botched, that millennial dreams are always dashed, and that man will surely be snuffed out, he can peer into the future—discerning, for example, that data processing and divination will merge by the year 2050. Can you do that?

The Libyan lion hunts no butterflies, and I won't stoop to pleading for your abstention from the Party of Pique. I refer to those cockamamie commandos of correctitude, those lefties in labels, who are bent on "expanding the canon"—that is, dismantling it. Success of all kinds is anathema to them, whether it be the fame of classic authors or the popularity of a critic who transmits sensible literary judgments to large numbers of culturally hungry fellow citizens whose heads are uncluttered by postmodernist claptrap.

The Party of Pique may well succeed, at least for a generation or two, in banishing from academic consideration the Western masters whose greatness irks them so: Chaucer, Shakespeare, Milton, Tirso de Molina, Adalbert Stifter,

Trumbull Stickney, Jones Very, A. A. Milne. Or, worse, they will keep those titans in nominal view while distorting them beyond all recognition. That would appear to be your current design upon poor Milne, and nothing I say here will prevent you from executing it.

I do, nevertheless, feel obliged to put on record my utter disdain for your vice of "explaining" masterpieces by stuffing them into the banal determinism of race, class, and gender. I defy all such attempted soul murder by adducing, as a puzzle for analysis, my own eccentric and inimitable self. Can you honestly contemplate Orpheus Bruno—this incongruous compendium of idiosyncrasy and genius housed within a sagging pile of sclerotic flesh—and maintain that he was "determined" by some congeries of cookie-cutter circumstances? Yet the meanest work of literature is no more unfathomable and irreducible than Bruno is.

Preeminent among your smelly little orthodoxies is the one to which we were all subjected a few minutes ago: militant feminism. After hearing such a harangue as Professor What's-her-name's, one must strain to remember that women at their best—the silent, beautiful ones that Yeats so admired—deserve comparison with the graces, the muses, the naiads and dryads. Moreover, there are women who can write with the best of men; one such prodigy will even figure in my argument here today. But academic feminists aren't women; they are harpies, demons from hell. I'm not so foolhardy as to spice their witches' brew by leaping into the cauldron myself. Rather, I withdraw discreetly from the scene, leaving the baritone banshees to judge for themselves how little satisfaction can be gleaned from endlessly "liberating" one another.

How cooling that your causes coalesce!
Excuse me, ladies, while I detumesce.

Well, perhaps a "methodological" object lesson is in order now. Let us consider the heraldic image of an amply proportioned Winnie-the-Pooh tiptoeing on a chair to reach a honey pot in his larder. If you've brought along an edition of *Pooh*, you may study the drawing itself on page 61 or thereabouts. What do you think you are seeing? If you were an earnest high school senior in AP English, you might translate this image into a kitschy allegory; it's a figure, say, of Aspiration. Being modish academics, though, you doubtless prefer an allegory drawn from your own sewing circle: the picture really bespeaks Commodity Fetishism, or Depletion of Natural Resources, or the Recycling of Social Energy, or, best of all, Male Rapacity. Your symbol hunting, don't you see, differs only trivially from that of the innocents who doze through your required courses and whom you despise without good reason.

Translation itself—the escape from literary presence to packaged significance—is precisely the error here. What you ought to be registering is a teddy bear stretching for a honey pot. To insist on further portent is to take a step backward in sophistication. It aligns soi-disant postmodernists with the invisible universe of Cotton Mather and the medieval fathers of the church, not with modern poetry's daring literalism, as exemplified in Williams's "I have eaten / the plums / that were in / the icebox."[1]

---

1. "This Is Just to Say," in *The Collected Poems of William Carlos Williams*, 2 vols., ed. A. Walton Litz and Christopher MacGowan (New York: New Directions, 1986), 1:372.

That breakthrough into the godless present moment was, of course, less a discovery than homage to the touchstone of all writerly merit: Shakespeare, who defied popes, bishops, and deconstructionists by unflinchingly holding the mirror up to nature. As does *Pooh*, which is to literature for the young what Shakespeare is to literature altogether. We do not explain *Pooh*; it explains us, through the sheer fullness of its represented life. It possesses no portable meaning that we can corrupt to our tawdry didactic ends; nor does it allow us to forget that artistic facts are always *willed*. "In poetry," Pooh tells Piglet, "—well, you *did* it, because the poetry says you did. And that's how people know." *There's* a wisdom far more radical than that of the neophyte Nietzscheans and Rolex revolutionaries who have seized control of the academy.

A strong author, like a strong critic, knows that the literary game isn't about making a living or teaching a lesson but about ensuring that we'll never be able to dispense with his brainchild. And the few very great ones can't resist rubbing their immortality in our faces. Shakespeare flaunts the fact that Prospero's cloud-capp'd towers, though made of the sheerest cardboard, will outlast every castle in England. So, too, there's no exaggeration in the final, startlingly boastful clause of *The House at Pooh Corner*: "a little boy and his Bear will always be playing." It's nothing but the truth—and centuries after your clamorous "isms" have faded into silence, the boy and the Bear will be playing yet.

Pooh, however, isn't Shakespearean merely in its stature. Awareness of Shakespeare's masterworks guides the author's hand in every chapter, adding nihilistic starch to the limp sentimentalities of the romper room. In chapter 4, for example, we encounter an unmistakable Hamlet surrogate. Like the dyspeptic prince, this character doesn't "seem to have felt at all how for a long time." Not technically a canine but distinctly hangdog in demeanor, he might almost be called a melancholy Great Dane. And just as his literary ancestor does, he manifests a depressive inability to take arms against a sea of troubles—into which he literally tumbles in one episode of unmitigated terror: "There was a loud splash, and Eeyore disappeared. . . ." That the "sea" in this instance is a sylvan stream only goes to show that Milne's imagination was caught up not only in Hamlet's plight but in the doomed Ophelia's as well.

Equally Shakespearean is Milne's boldly lifelike departure from the most sacred convention of juvenile fiction, the happy ending. No more in *The House at Pooh Corner* than in *King Lear* do we find the hero repaid with good fortune for his admirable traits and for the many indignities he has been made to suffer. Lear dies, heartbroken, over the corpse of Cordelia. Pooh will be unceremoniously tossed into an attic by some domestic factotum as Christopher Robin, putting away childish things, looks ahead to the well-known stages of English character building: schoolwork, spanking, sodomy, self-abuse, and eventual espousal to a bucktoothed stick.

Everybody loathes a goody-goody mama's boy, as I learned the hard way at Music and Art. That's why you won't see any Christopher Robin T-shirts or picnic napkins out there in the real world, where Pooh spectacularly reigns. It is Pooh, not the privileged, self-advancing, all too socializable Christopher, who has earned our lifelong affection. And yet we perceive with stark clarity that Christopher, not Pooh, will be the survivor here. It doesn't seem fair to a Friendly Bear—does it, now, my dears?—to throw him away like a broken chair.

For those of you who have actually taken the trouble to read some Shakespeare, doesn't this rough treatment ring another bell—specifically, from *2 Henry IV*? Without a doubt, Christopher Robin amounts to a reworking of the suddenly sober Prince Hal, who dismisses his dearest friend so that he can rule without encumbrance from his lawless past. Pooh, then, is twin to that very friend—a character meant to embody the fun-loving plenitude that will be shamefully sacrificed to his ex-companion's worldly ambition. He's a reincarnation, in fur and stuffing, of the most profoundly human and sympathetic personage ever drawn by Shakespeare or by anyone else, John Falstaff.

The first hint of this doppelgänger role is offered early in *Winnie-the-Pooh*, when the admirable bear is said to have completed his morning Stoutness Exercises. Not, *nota bene*, his Slimming Exercises. This animal is trying to get even fatter than he already is. It can't be because he is preparing to hibernate; that's the one form of inactivity in which he doesn't indulge. The only conceivable explanation is that Pooh is bulking up to qualify as the twentieth century's own plump Jack.

It's no coincidence that the most rotund, characterologically speaking, of figures in world literature is also among the weightiest of flesh. Shakespeare knew just what he was doing in lending mountainous avoirdupois to his immortal highwayman, slacker, and wastrel. A number of Shepard's drawings give us, in fact, precisely a new Falstaff, burping with mere indigestion, not guilt, as he returns to semialertness after a typically immodest and self-absorbed feat of gourmandise. And lest we miss the point, Milne goes out of his way to get his continually feasting protagonist knighted as Sir Pooh de Bear, now a social as well as a physical dead ringer for his obese fore*bear* Sir John Falstaff.

Winnie-the-Pooh, I must emphasize, does not contain Shakespearean "meanings"; it contains Shakespeare himself as a ghostly but animating tenant. And a critic steeped in the Western canon, lovingly bending his ear to the text, can hear other precursor voices as well. There is, for example, the later Henry James:

> "Well?" said Rabbit.
>
> "Yes," said Owl, looking Wise and Thoughtful. "I see what you mean. Undoubtedly."
>
> "Well?"
>
> "Exactly," said Owl. "Precisely." And he added, after a little thought, "If you had not come to me, I should have come to you."
>
> "Why?" asked Rabbit.
>
> "For that very reason," said Owl, hoping that something helpful would happen soon.

If such echoes were only a curiosity, lacking dynamic import in the formation of Milne's literary self, you could be forgiven for taking no interest in them. Long ago, however, I demonstrated that every strong author *overcomes* his most imposing predecessors by introjecting them in subtly demeaning ways. The Tardive, or latecomer, clears space for his claim upon posterity by implicitly undermining the Earlybird whose stature would otherwise eclipse him. Thus, by putting his own Prince Hal in short pants and by reducing his Falstaff to a mere teddy bear, Milne shows that he won't be intimidated by the pomp and circumstance of *2 Henry IV*. And by subtracting the already minuscule speck of psychological matter around which a late-Jamesian conversation maddeningly orbits, he parodically needles the Master (who might otherwise have left him feeling preempted) as a spinner of dialogue that portentously arrives nowhere.

But James is by no means, for Milne, the most important post-Shakespearean Earlybird. Since *Pooh* features a nature-loving forest child (Christopher) and a rhapsodizing poet-protagonist (Pooh), Milne knows that he is going *mano a mano* here with the premier celebrator both of infant sagacity and of the inherently poetical character of routine experience. Not for nothing does he begin the preface to *When We Were Very Young* by invoking "Mr. William Wordsworth" and seeking to distinguish his own practice from the giant ancestor's. Quite simply, recasting Wordsworth as a deluded bore is the most urgent project of the entire four-book cluster.[2]

In view of its ending, *The House at Pooh Corner* could appropriately have taken as an epigraph Wordsworth's lament, in his "Intimations" ode, "Shades of the prison-house begin to close / Upon the growing Boy." Yet the same poem, when it rashly declares that children are born trailing clouds of glory from a spirit realm, gives Milne the opening he needs to squelch his daunting rival. He "refutes" Wordsworth by making sure that the *Pooh* characters won't be even minimally intelligent, much less suffused with a preexistent divine wisdom. Likewise, he pointedly deflates Wordsworthian communion with nature by seeing to it that Pooh's spontaneous

---

2. Milne must have anticipated this fight to the finish years before sitting down to compose *Pooh*. Why else would he have married Dorothy (he called her Daphne) de Selincourt, a woman he scarcely liked and would soon despise? The de Selincourts happened to be the first family of Wordsworth scholarship, and Milne must have reasoned that in exchange for constant domestic annoyance, he would get an insider's view of everything that was wrong with his Romantic nemesis.

verses ("Sing Ho! for a Bear! / Sing Ho! for a Pooh!") never reach beyond the bounds of impercipient narcissism.

Moreover, Milne saucily endows the dismissible Piglet with Wordsworth's own penchant for contemplating flowers in a dreamy, speculative, wishful mood:

> The Piglet was sitting on the ground at the door of his house blowing happily at a dandelion, and wondering whether it would be this year, next year, sometime or never. He had just discovered that it would be never, and he was trying to remember what "*it*" was, hoping it wasn't anything nice, when Pooh came up.

Nothing at all, we are left to infer, can be retrieved from prenatal existence or deciphered from nature's chaotic lesson book. Like W. C. Williams after him, Milne insists that a dandelion remains just a weed, not a portal between the phenomenal and noumenal worlds. And thus Wordsworth, the botanizing transcendentalist, is made to look like a fool who can't content himself with the insignificance that quite suffices to fill Pooh's and Piglet's *très riches heures*.

So much, then, for the major influences and Milne's cunning means of containing them. Assembling the total picture, what do we see—a work of narrow bourgeois smugness? You may think so, but that's because you fail to understand that Milne's struggle against authority—no deference to literary masters, no groveling before priests and preachers—is Promethean or even Satanic in scale. The truth is that heroic blasphemy, not complacency, is the ruling principle of this book and the key to its ultimate greatness.

Milne would not have repeatedly called Pooh's forest "enchanted" if he hadn't wanted us to compare it to the paradise of Scripture. Just think: the author/God of *Pooh* sends his only begotten son, *Christ*opher, into a world where no fall has occurred, no sin requires atonement, and no apocalyptic end to history is contemplated, because history proves to be only an endless round of inconsequential neighborly exchanges. Surely this is sacrilegious satire, a cunning inversion of Judeo-Christian belief in a Messiah who will settle all accounts with sinners (bad) and obedient cowards (good). If so, Milne deserves to be ranked not with Beatrix Potter and Dr. Seuss but with our finest heretics—with the Gnostic Valentinus, the Kabbalist Moses Cordovero, the Sufi Ibn al-'Arabi, the Shi'ite al-Hallaj, and, if you must know, with their modern avatar, Orpheus Bruno.

As soon as Milne has been placed in this noble company, however, a biographical misgiving that has been nagging at me all along becomes an insuperable problem. Can we accept that the triumphant diabolism of *Pooh* was really achieved by a light-verse hack for *Punch* and the author of third-rate drawing-room plays? And could that same featherweight have made Pooh into the most beloved character, but for Falstaff himself, in all of world literature? The same intuitive power—and it has never failed me yet—that first put me onto "Milne's" kinship with God-spurning alchemists, necromancers, and theosophists now tells me that we may have been the victims of a colossal trick. Who, we must ask, *really* wrote *Winnie-the-Pooh*?

Among Milne's contemporaries, very few meet the triple criteria for authorship of *Pooh*: metaphysical pessimism, extraordinary literary gifts, and a knack for writing sympathetically about animal characters. There is, of course, Franz Kafka, a worthy candidate in all three respects. I judge, however, that the gap between Gregor Samsa on the one hand

and Alexander Beetle on the other is too vast to be plausibly bridged. A better fit—even, perhaps, a perfect fit—is provided by an author who wrote fluently in Milne's own tongue, who lived conveniently nearby, and who, uniquely in English literature, produced a book-length biography of a cocker spaniel. I refer to Virginia Woolf, author of *Flush*, whose other masterpiece, *To the Lighthouse*, was published just one year after *Winnie-the-Pooh*.

We can test our hypothesis by examining *To the Lighthouse* for signs of a deep, inimitable identity with the mind that created *Pooh*. The key practical issue of Woolf's novel is whether the Ramsays will find fair enough weather for a sailing jaunt to visit a lighthouse keeper. In insisting that a predicted storm will make the trip impossible, Mr. Ramsay is obviously echoing Eeyore's forecast: "It will rain soon, you see if it doesn't." And when, eventually, the old widower and his grown son James do make it to the lighthouse in a small boat, Woolf would seem to be shamelessly recycling the water voyage that she had employed, a year before, to carry Christopher Robin and Pooh to a cathartic rendezvous of their own with the stranded Piglet:

> "We might go in your umbrella," said Pooh. . . .
>   "I shall call this boat *The Brain of Pooh*," said Christopher Robin, and *The Brain of Pooh* set sail forthwith in a south-westerly direction, revolving gracefully.

Isn't it probable, then, that Woolf surreptitiously wrote the *Pooh* books and colluded with Milne to enhance his reputation while preserving hers from infantilization?

You may wonder, as I myself have, why Woolf would have proposed such a scheme to the nobody Milne, of all people. Well, I've already shown that the author of *Pooh* was a devotee of mystic codes and correspondences. Woolf must have noticed that the name A. A. Milne contains anagrams for IN A MALE, pointing to a provisional sex change for the androgynous author of *Orlando*; I AM LEAN, indicating Woolf's chronic emaciation; and MANILA E, a clue that may someday lead investigators to the envelope in which she made a full confession of the ruse. In that case, mere thematic thrift, not influence, would explain why climatic disturbance and aquatic adventure figure so prominently in both fictions. At the same time, a bipolar, borderline psychotic Tardive author such as Woolf, who must have already envied the public's adulation of *When We Were Very Young*, could have devised no more foolproof strategy for coping with the menace of *Pooh*'s imminent greatness than to take pen in hand and write the book herself.

Short of dusting off my old Ouija board and trying to call up the shades of Woolf and Milne, I see no quick way of determining for sure which of them penned *Winnie-the-Pooh*. My gnostic insight favors Woolf, but my equally clamorous rational faculty is troubled by some awkward biographical details, such as the fact that A. A. Milne used to tell stories about a certain Pooh Bear to a son named Christopher Robin, who, remarkably enough, possessed a teddy bear with that very name.[3] It's a toss-up, really. All I can do—and I expect to

---

3. A further question is why a Poohless Milne would have bothered to marry into the de Selincourt clan (note 2 above). But the difficulty vanishes if we suppose that the *idea* for *Winnie-the-Pooh* as an exercise in anti-Wordsworthian countersublimity did originate with Milne. He could have mentioned his scheme to Woolf, who would have been at once amused by his clumsy presumption and intrigued by the prospect of nursing this initial spark into the eternal flame that is *Pooh*.

spend every waking moment of the next two months on this project—is to write two books on the issue, taking opposite stands, and let the world decide which of them is more convincing.

But does it matter, in the last analysis? Pooh's greatness—I mean that of Winnie-the-Pooh himself as an immortal personage—reaches both forward and back in time, summoning kindred spirits to his side. And they come when they are called. In my mind's eye I see three exceptional souls—Falstaff, Pooh, Bruno!—standing together and towering over their respective epochs like the triple pillars of the world.

We three may seem at first an unlikely grouping, because I am the only Neoplatonic visionary among us. But deeper down, we share a contentment within our lumpish bodies, an indifference to allegedly noble causes, and an instinctive resistance to hypocrisy and pretension of every kind. The academy's prefabricated analyses and its me-too ideologizing shrink away in the presence of our unapologetic, well-merited self-admiration. If you could grasp the import of the following exchange—*really* grasp it, as countless ordinary readers have done with my encouragement—you might be able to leave your fashionable shibboleths behind:

"Oh, Bear!" said Christopher Robin. "How I do love you!"

"So do I," said Pooh.

CHAPTER SIX

Resident Aliens

DAS NUFFA DAT

Born and raised in a suburb of Calcutta, Das N. Dat received his earliest training at the hands of tutors, who recommended that he continue his education in England. Distinguishing himself at Eton and then at Oxford (A.B. 1974, D.Phil. 1979), Dat went on to become a pioneer of Postcolonial Studies. His fame rests on essays—originally conference papers delivered in sites as various as Tel Aviv, Bloomington, Christchurch, and Prague—that exerted a shaping influence on his young field long before they were collected in 1995 as *Diaspora to Nowhere: Dislocation and the Nonsemiotics of Unbelonging*.

After stints of acclaimed teaching in Australia, Canada, and Scotland, Dat recently accepted the coveted title Classic Coke Professor of Subaltern Studies at Emory University. "With this appointment," as Emory's president declared in a press release, "marginality now takes center stage at Emory."

———

"Sometimes," said Eeyore, "when people have quite finished taking a person's house, there are one or two bits which they don't want and are rather glad for the person to take back, if you know what I mean."

THIS is an hour, my friends, to which I have looked forward more avidly than you will easily be willing to credit. Though our topic—the traces of a great historic crime as found in one modern writer's work—is one that could well divide us along ethnic and national lines, I feel, instead, the warmest bond of amity with you decent and dedicated cultural labourers. We have so much to discuss! For, as Gayatri Chakravorty Spivak has said so well, "The rememoration of the 'present' as space is the possibility of the utopian imperative of no-(particular)-place, the metropolitan project that can supplement the post-colonial attempt at the impossible cathexis of place-bound history as the lost time of the spectator."[1] That's what we're all here for, wouldn't you agree?

I especially welcome the opportunity to renew cordial ties with those of my fellow panelists who happen to be friends of long standing. Victor Fassell, *primus inter pares*! I'm sure, Vic, that you share my cherished recollection of the larks we had at university when you were a fresh young Rhodes scholar and I, younger still, had recently come up from Eton, perhaps too single-mindedly bent upon the First

———

1. Gayatri Chakravorty Spivak, "Psychoanalysis in Left Field and Fieldworking: Examples to Fit the Title," in *Speculations after Freud: Psychoanalysis, Philosophy, and Culture*, ed. Sonu Shamdasani and Michael Münchow (London and New York: Routledge, 1994), p. 63.

that I was eventually fortunate enough to receive. The ideal antidote to such overweening academicism was punting on the Thames with you, Vic, and catching one another up on the finer points of cricket, rugger, and high tea.

Vic and I amicably part company, however, over Foucault, a well-meaning but parochial bloke whose paradigmatic European prison and asylum cannot begin to explain how a despised indigeneity gets catachrestically imbricated in a dominant. Nor, I maintain, ought we to be playing ducks and drakes with the Marxian conceptions that Miss Carla Gulag so pluckily defended earlier today. Where, I must ask, was Marx's benign Dialectic when thousands of my countrymen were slaughtered during the Great Mutiny? Granted, "materialist as classificatory work seeks both ontogenetic rifts and their renegotiations."[2] Yet "the event of representation as *Vertretung* (in the constellation of rhetoric-as-persuasion) behaves like a *Darstellung* (or rhetoric-as-trope), taking its place in the gap between the formation of a (descriptive) class and the nonformation of a (transformative) class."[3] With all deference to the charming Miss Gulag, then, I think we must insist on a more concrete mode of inquiry, purged of essentialist abstractions.

Ironically, I must add, class-conscious Marxist thinkers appear to take little heed of the alien peons within their midst. Although, for example, we were all entertained by

2. Mike Hill, "Vipers in Shangri-la: Whiteness, Writing, and Other Ordinary Terrors," introduction to *Whiteness: A Critical Reader*, ed. Mike Hill (New York and London: New York Univ. Press, 1997), p. 11.

3. Gayatri Chakravorty Spivak, "Can the Subaltern Speak? Speculations on Widow-Sacrifice," in *Marxism and the Interpretation of Culture*, ed. Cary Nelson and Lawrence Grossberg (Basingstoke: Macmillan Education, 1988), p. 277.

Fredric Jameson's deconstruction of the postmodern Bonaventure Hotel, as recounted by Miss Gulag, I gather that
Jameson looked straight past the ethnic and migrant infra-
structure that, labouring in the hidden kitchens and laundry
rooms of such hotels, renders them virtual colonies in their
own right. I say, his discussion might have been more culturally sensitive if, as I once did, he had rented a Bonaventure
suite for a fortnight and noted the lamentable self-abasement
of the room service personnel.

Our outgoing MLA president, Edward Said, did not
exaggerate, I fear, when he declared that "every European, in
what he could say about the Orient, was . . . a racist, an
imperialist, and almost totally ethnocentric."[4] Even the
most eminent of French Orientalists, Louis Massignon, was
exposed by Said as merely "a kind of system for producing
certain kinds of statements, disseminated into the large mass
of discursive formations that together make up the archive,
or cultural material of his time."[5] Why, the bounder was
scarcely a person at all! Happily, though, we who have gathered today *are* persons, and deeply caring ones. And what we
presently care about is seeing whether a rigorous postcolonial hermeneutic can afford us a nonracist, nonchauvinist
purchase on the major writings of A. A. Milne.

You are doubtless hoping (generous souls that you are)
that I will absolve the beloved Milne of any association with
the crimes and cruelties of empire. After all, the fellow is well
known to have been a pacifist in the period between the two
world wars. Straight off, however, I must let the penny drop.

---

4. Edward Said, *Orientalism* (New York: Pantheon, 1978), p. 204.
5. Said, *Orientalism*, p. 274.

To up sticks and embrace pacifism in the twenties, when the imperial row of dominoes was beginning to teeter before all discerning eyes, was simply to deny one's obvious complicity in the extortion of wealth from victim lands. And this is precisely what we find, among other harrowing yet predictable revelations, when we turn to Milne's various writings in prose and verse for his pampered son and other apprentice sahibs.

In one of his poems Milne tells those impressionable children:

> *Don't be afraid of doing things.*
> (Especially, of course, for Kings.)

Milne even dares to fancy *himself* an imperial ruler who can enlist the dark-skinned natives in satisfying his perverse tastes:

> If I were King of Timbuctoo,
> I'd think of lovely things to do.

And with Britannia still ruling the waves in the loot-laden twenties, dreams of endless conquest proved as irresistible to Milne as to John Bull in general. Sailing his chimerical ship "through Eastern seas" and taking possession of whatever island struck his fancy,

> I'd say to myself as I looked so lazily down at the sea:
> "There's nobody else in the world, and the world was made
> for me."

Here is Western solipsism in its most grandiose and ominous mood. "There's nobody else in the world"? You're off by quite a stretch, A.A., old chum. For one thing, there's the problem of having to contend with fellow imperialists from rival European nations. Mussolini, for example, who had come to power in 1922, was already casting covetous eyes on North Africa when Milne, perhaps anticipating a clash of territorial claims between Italy and England, wrote, "They went out hunting, and they caught three wopses."

Though killing a few unarmed Italians may be jolly sport, a face-off with third worlders in their own forests and jungles would be a stickier wicket altogether. Milne offers us a number of stanzas that place a British voyager—himself, thinly disguised—in harm's way as he strives to hold down a mounting panic. What if the island he has assumed to be uninhabited actually teems with "savages"?

> Sitting safe in his hut he'd have nothing to fear,
> Whereas now they might suddenly breathe in his ear!

The horror, the horror!—namely, of coming face-to-face with some of the people who already live in peace with the surroundings that one is dashed-all bent upon despoiling.

Hearing the tom-toms getting louder as he longs to be back in his country manor sipping amontillado and reading *Blackwood's* at the fireside, what can a stout Englishman like Milne do but try to switch off his terrified imagination? The effort of banishment to the unconscious is especially evident in the queasy poem "Nursery Chairs," in which Milne conceives of himself as leading his "faithful band" up the Amazon River. Ominously, "Indians in twos and threes" begin clustering on the banks. But is he worried? Not a bit of it! Why, with English *sang-froid* he will simply wave his hand,

And then they turn and go away—
They always understand.

Don't they, though—but I wouldn't wager a farthing on it if I were you. In the real world, daft apotropaic verses of this kind can do precious little to stay the arching bows and poison-tipped arrows of traduced but not yet conquered tribesmen.

It can't be an accident that Milne's prototypical subalterns are characterised as "Indians." For a Britisher who has been weaned on colonialist propaganda, all Indians are alike, and they're all from Asia. You surely won't have forgotten Milne's poem about bad King John, whose yearned-for *India* rubber ball arrives out of the blue from a Santa Claus whose worker-elves would hardly have been growing their own rubber in the Arctic Circle. Less conspicuously, but even more tellingly, we learn from the concluding chapter of *Winnie-the-Pooh* that India rubber—which, remember, is nothing but booty pinched from Sumatra and other "Indies"—works well "for rubbing out anything which you had spelt wrong." Isn't this a trope for repression, and specifically for repression of what "trade" with South Asia was actually like? If so, we can expect that *Pooh* itself, which cannot fail to show the same politicocognitive limitations as the poems, will have India and the Indies constantly tugging at its guilty conscience.

But a nationalist freedom fighter such as myself—one who inhaled a staunch Fabianism from his natal soil of Bengal—cannot turn blithely to analysis of *Pooh* without first coping with a grave misgiving. As my grandfather the maharajah never tired of pointing out, the founding moment of "English" as an academic field occurred when the imperialist historian Thomas Macaulay brazenly urged that Indians be rendered "English in taste, in opinions, in morals, and in intellect" through compulsory exposure to *his* nation's literature.[6] A rum job, that. As the most widely read modern text in the master tongue—a text, moreover, that we shall find more indoctrinating than most—*Pooh* continues to serve Macaulay's program not just in India but everywhere. How, then, can I presume to discuss it without swelling its pernicious influence even further?

A possible riposte could be that one neutralises *Pooh*'s ideological effect in the very act of exposing and denouncing it. That's one up on the Empire, true enough, and I shall be doing a spot of such neutralising myself in just a twinkling. Yet the mode of indignant alarm wears precious thin after a while. If, instead, we make full use of *postmodern* postcolonial conceptions—among others, "aporia, ambivalence, indeterminacy, the question of discursive closure, the threat to agency, the status of intentionality, the challenge to 'totalizing' concepts"[7]—our critique can be immeasurably more efficacious, even revolutionary.

You will have to brace yourselves for some psychological complexities if we are to avoid confusion here. On its face, *Winnie-the-Pooh* is a harmless tissue of twaddle about a teddy bear, and that's what Milne, the dithering twit, thought he was writing. Beneath the surface, however, we will find the

---

6. Thomas Babington Macaulay, "Minute on Indian Education," in *Selected Writings*, ed. John Clive and Thomas Pinney (Chicago: Univ. of Chicago Press, 1972), p. 249.
7. Homi K. Bhabha, *The Location of Culture* (London and New York: Routledge, 1994), p. 173.

same unabashed loyalty to imperialist values already noted in his poems. That subliminal message—the sun ought never to set on England's far-flung property—is the work of Milne's Colonial Unconscious. But because the oppressor must always try, only half successfully, to stifle a sympathy with the oppressed, there's a second homunculus, the rebellious *Colonised* Unconscious, who has taken up subversive residence within the first one. And if our interpretative efforts can give voice to this Colonised Unconscious, we will have unchained a virtual Spartacus. By bringing to light the text's own lurking counterhegemonic impulses, postmodern postcolonial criticism can show just where the self-divided "master" psyche is most vulnerable to paralysis from within.

Methodological sophistication is especially imperative for unpacking *Winnie-the-Pooh*, because the book's symbolic locus is curiously dual. Instead of directly treating the British Empire and the brutalisation of its subjects, *Pooh* introduces us to anthropomorphic animals who mind one another's business in some sylvan backwater of Albion. But as soon as we open the book and confront a *map*—the signature icon of predatory colonial "expotitions"—we know that we'll be watching what Homi K. Bhabha has called "the colonial space played out in the imaginative geography of the metropolitan space."[8] And this means that a critic must stay alert for the faintest cryptic hints of East-West polarisation, immigrant-emigrant chiasmus, and subterranean struggle between the Colonial and Colonised Unconsciouses.

The subaltern foreign presence, though thematically quiescent, looms everywhere in *Pooh*. I refer above all to those

---

8. Bhabha, *Location*, p. 168.

negligible hordes imported, one might fancy, straight from Calcutta or Bombay: Rabbit's friends and relations, who "spread themselves about on the grass, and waited hopefully in case anybody spoke to them, or dropped anything, or asked them the time." Descending from mice through frogs to myriad insects ripe for squashing, these repulsive creatures follow by just two years the endless parade of Indians, animals, bugs, and microbes that in *A Passage to India* are deemed too numerous for admission to the Christian heaven, lest nothing be left there for God's chosen English to enjoy. As good professing liberals, both Milne and Forster would plead ironic distance from that sentiment, but their visceral attachment to the full colonial shilling is all too patent.

Of course, India alone cannot absorb the sum total of Milne's lust for flag planting. Just before entering stage right in *The House at Pooh Corner*, Christopher Robin is said to have "spent the morning indoors going to Africa and back." No finer way to greet the dawn, eh what, than by bagging a few fictive rhinos in Kenya or "Rhodesia"—accompanied, you can be sure, by muscular near-naked "savages" in bulging loincloths who will bear one's litter, serve one's Cadbury's Cottage Chocs on a silver tray, and extract the horns of the slaughtered beasts for powdered aphrodisiacs that can be sold to gullible oldsters in "Oriental" chemistry shops.

But Milne's Colonised Unconscious cannot sit idly by while *Pooh* goes about rejoicing in the state's piratic criminality. A native uprising is imperative. In this light, consider the very first episode of *Winnie-the-Pooh*, in which the overfed but insatiable protagonist—a veritable Colonel Blimp who will later be knighted and officially decorated as "F.O.P. (Friend of Piglet's), R.C. (Rabbit's Companion), P.D. (Pole

Discoverer), E.C. and T.F. (Eeyore's Comforter and Tail-finder)"—attempts to steal honey from a tree-borne bees' nest without being noticed:

> "It's like this," he said. "When you go after honey with a balloon, the great thing is not to let the bees know you're coming. . . . I shall try to look like a small black cloud. That will deceive them."

Like an agent of the East India Company hoping to trade pence-apiece spools of yarn for precious spices, the marauder supposes that the provincial horde or swarm will be gulled by any pretense on his part—even that a bear suspended beneath a balloon is merely a passing cloud.

Alas for Milne's hero, the indigenes are found to be "*the wrong sort of bees*"—or rather, just the right sort, top-hole lads who, metaphorically speaking, have been rallied to militancy by Aimé Césaire and Frantz Fanon. And because Pooh must *blacken* himself for camouflage, we can infer that the bees themselves are black. They are the dauntless "Africanised" variety that would later send shivers up the spine of negrophobes on your own blood-drenched, history-haunted continent.[9] It would appear, then, that *Pooh*'s Colonised Unconscious has in view here the most humiliating of all

---

9. A justly outraged scholar has alerted us to one such incident of racialist panic in the flimsy guise of concern over public health: "Last month, a Tucson radio station reported that after a summer of near-fatal attacks by the so-called 'Africanized Bees,' these 'Killer' bees are being successfully captured and removed to yield a place for 'the benign European honey bees.' *Rituals of exclusivity and stigmatization are exercised daily.*" Joan Dayan, "'A Receptacle for That Race of Men': Blood, Boundaries, and Mutations of Theory," *American Literature* 67 (1995), p. 810; emphasis added.

setbacks incurred by British imperialism, the donnybrook at Khartoum in 1885.[10]

Needless to say, Milne's *Colonial* Unconscious cherishes quite a different aim. Through dear old clubbable Pooh, Milne is saying to young captives of the Empire, "Calm yourselves! Instead of risking massacre by trigger-happy Tommies, why not just drop into your neighbor's hovel, open an expensive little tin of something from the 'mother country,' and have a nice chat about the weather?" But the discerning critic, attuned to "hybridity as camouflage, as a contesting, antagonistic agency functioning in the time-lag of sign/symbol which is a space in-between the rules of engagement,"[11] can see that Pooh himself is a psychological hybrid—a would-be overlord whose will has been sapped by subliminal identification with the very subjects he has subjugated.

"The *anti-dialectical* movement of the subaltern instance," as Bhabha explains, "subverts any binary or sublatory ordering of power and sign; it defers the object of the look . . . and endows it with a strategic motion, which we may here, analogously, name the movement of the death drive."[12] *It defers the object of the look*: think about this, won't you? If the enabling fetish of colonialism is an image of the subhuman native,

---

10. Is Pooh Gordon, then, or is he Kitchener? A bit of both, I'd say. It was Gordon who was literally brought to earth at Khartoum, but Pooh's strategy of trying to *distract* the bees brings to mind the canny but frustrated Kitchener. "His idea," says the sycophantic *Encyclopaedia Britannica* of Egypt's one-time consul general, "was to keep the country busy with the contemplation of its own affairs" (1947 ed., 13:419).

11. Homi K. Bhabha, "Postcolonial Authority and Postmodern Guilt," in *Cultural Studies*, ed. Lawrence Grossberg, Cary Nelson, and Paula A. Treichler (New York and London: Routledge, 1992), p. 63.

12. Bhabha, *Location*, p. 55.

then the dichotomising impulse that constructs him as such is disabled when the colonial master, gazing into his looking glass—itself a mere shard in this instance—must confront the pathetic fragmentation of his own psyche.

This is no phantasy on my part; the picture itself awaits your own gaze on page 146 of *Pooh*. Here Pooh Bear—or shouldn't we rather say Poo-Bah?—suddenly face-to-face with his brutish self, struggles against a masochistic urge, emanating precisely from his guilt-inflamed death drive, to crush his swelled head from either side with two stiff floor-polishing brushes that a disaffected and defiant native servant must have left lying about his headquarters.

Standing disconsolate before the glass, Pooh has been launched, willy-nilly, into Lacan's Mirror Phase—which is to say that self-absence and castration fear will henceforth hound and cripple him. All that remains to him, we can infer from Lacanian/Kristevan/Deleuzoguattarian theory, is his desire. But desire for what? Beating a coolie, extorting sexual favors from a starving petitioner, playing a round of croquet with Adela Quested? No, all that is behind him now. He is adrift with the terrible knowledge that desire itself is self-reflexive, at once vacant and complete.[13]

---

13. As Deleuze and Guattari put it: "Desire does not lack anything; it does not lack its object. It is, rather, the subject that is lacking in desire, or desire that lacks a fixed subject; there is no fixed subject except by repression. Desire and its object are a unity; it is the machine, as a machine of a machine. Desire is machine, the object of desire also a connected machine, so that the product is lifted from the process of producing, and something detaches itself from producing to product and gives a leftover to the vagabond, nomad subject." Gilles Deleuze and Félix Guattari, *Anti-Oedipus: Capitalism and Schizophrenia*, trans. Richard Hurley et al. (New York: Viking, 1977), p. 26.

If Pooh is always already inhibited in the in-betweenness of his logomotion; if his every cell is infested by the foreign socius he has failed to subdue; if, in brief, the would-be bully has been self-stymied on what Spivak has called "the preontological ontic level of the everydayness of the being"[14]—then we needn't, after all, get in a paddy about the ideological harm he can wreak on young third-world readers. In fact, we really needn't do anything at all. As you've seen, the Colonised Unconscious has already had its way with both Pooh and Milne, turning their backbones to Yorkshire pudding.

I shall leave you, though, with one extended reflection of a more intimate nature. Ideally, I am all too aware, my resistant, transgressive analysis of *Pooh* ought to have been conducted by some peasant subaltern who, still trapped within his occupied homeland, daily feels the lash of imperialism still more keenly than I do. Unfortunately, however, as Gayatri Spivak has shown, even without the intimidation of an imperial overseer the subaltern simply cannot speak.[15] Spivak proved the point by focusing on Indian widows who, until the meddlesome Brits forbade the custom in 1829, were required to be burned alive on their dead husbands' pyres. Sure enough, the resultant charred corpses were quite disempowered for analysing the nation's woe; in Ania Loomba's starkly observant phrase, they were "absent as subjects."[16]

---

14. Gayatri Chakravorty Spivak, *Outside in the Teaching Machine* (New York and London: Routledge, 1993), p. 37.

15. See Spivak, "Can the Subaltern Speak?"

16. Ania Loomba, *Colonialism/Postcolonialism* (London and New York: Routledge, 1998), p. 234.

So too, in the aggregate, are their modern counterparts, the multitudes now crammed so unhygienically along the banks of the Ganges. I have seen them up close, pressing against the windows of my father's Bentley. They are not so ready as you might suppose to practise the "sly civility" that Bhabha finds to be the native's most potent means of deflecting racist animus and forestalling discursive closure. Nor can they quite understand, as Bhabha does, that "the colonial hybrid is the articulation of the ambivalent space where the rite of power is enacted on the site of desire, making its objects at once disciplinary and disseminatory."[17] If they could think and talk like that, they wouldn't be just milling about all the time, now, would they?

It's evident, then, that tragically displaced cosmopolitan intellectuals such as Spivak, Bhabha, Loomba, and I must step in to speak *for* the immolated or otherwise muted subaltern. Each of us declares, with our compatriot Himani Bannerji, "I am offering up piece by piece my experience, body, intellect, so others can learn."[18] Of course those others include the subaltern, at least technically so. But in all candour, it's no small task trying to get and keep the blighter's attention, much less direct it to the interstices of a thorny text such as *Pooh*.

For the nonce, then, we must address ourselves to you MLA stalwarts—you who can grasp the idiom of postmodern postcoloniality and appreciate its awesome insurrectionary

---

17. Bhabha, *Location*, p. 112.
18. Himani Bannerji, "Re: Turning the Gaze," in *Beyond Political Correctness: Toward the Inclusive University*, ed. Stephen Richer and Lorna Weir (Toronto: Univ. of Toronto Press, 1995), p. 224.

power. We count upon you to pass the word along until it reaches all the way down to your own subalterns in Topeka and similar desolate wastes. If the ravages of imperialism are ever to end—if the colonising Heffalump one day lies down with the formerly colonised lamb—history may record that the first tremor of productive change was felt here, today, as we dear friends and scholars recontextualised a mere space of interrogation as a veritable site of intervention and, dare I say it, of contestation as well.

CHAPTER SEVEN

Gene/Meme Covariation in Ashdown Forest: Pooh and the Consilience of Knowledge

RENEE FRANCIS

From the outset of her academic career, Renee Francis has specialized in the application of scientific rigor to the study of children's literature. In her graduate work at the University of Missouri-St. Louis, she produced seminar papers—for example, "Rodent Nesting Hygiene in *The Tale of Mrs. Tittlemouse*" and "Monkey Business: *Curious George* and the Rhesus Mischief-Reconciliation Routine"—that saw publication even before she had completed her dissertation, "*Pat the Bunny* and the Opposable Hominid Thumb."

At Hobart and William Smith Colleges, where she assumed an assistant professorship in 1994, Francis became known for advocacy of unpopular views, some of which are reflected in the following outspoken paper. Like inferior species in the struggle for fitness, she maintained, second-rate professors and whole departments deserve to "go extinct," allowing the academic ecosystem to evolve more rapidly toward a vital cross-fertilization between the humanities and the sciences.

As of the academic year 2001–2002, Francis has embarked on a new career in Washington, D.C., as a clerk in the National Bureau of Standards.

FELLOW gene vehicles: I greet you at a momentous juncture in the human knowledge enterprise, in *Pooh* studies, and in the increasingly disgraceful history of academic literary criticism. And I won't mince words here. As many of you privately acknowledge, for the past two decades we've been enduring what Robert Storey has aptly called "the strained ingenuities, the political sophistries, the uncritical obeisances to fashionable authority that now corrupt the practices of the profession."[1] But shoddy work can be sent packing if scholars reach a common understanding of what went wrong; and the hour for such agreement has arrived at last.

Joseph Carroll—a leading figure, as is Storey, in the emergent and already formidable field of Biopoetics—has laid bare the faulty premises that you can now join me in repudiating:

By taking Derridean semiotics and Foucauldian discourse theory as a matrix within which to synthesize

---

1. Robert Storey, *Mimesis and the Human Animal: On the Biogenetic Foundations of Literary Representation* (Evanston: Northwestern Univ. Press, 1996), p. xvi.

the obsolete linguistics of Saussure and Jakobson, the obsolete psychology of Freud, and the obsolete sociology of Marx, poststructuralism has generated an ever more complex system of rhetoric altogether detached from empirical study.[2]

Empirical study—that's the ideal to which we can return if we muster the necessary will. And there's no better place to start than with *Winnie-the-Pooh* and *The House at Pooh Corner*, which have been systematically misconstrued by every one of my predecessors on this podium.

These works don't just deserve, like all others, to be accurately represented; they are *about* the importance of getting one's facts and theories straight. Each of Milne's chapters is a story told to his son for the latter's edification—a process that reaches a logical climax when, at the end, Christopher Robin tests out of home tutoring and into school per se. Yet to hear my postmodernist colleagues tell it, the wicked Pied Piper of Logocentrism is luring the boy away from a poetical state of ignorance, innumeracy, and bad spelling that ought to be prolonged through adolescence, maturity, and even senility, so that arid Reason can be permanently kept at bay.

In real life—and yes, Virginia, there is such a thing, it's not a "construct" or a "discourse"—Milne's son proved himself an eager pupil, especially in the master discipline of mathematics. And in doing so, he was following his father's own early path. The *Pooh* stories were written by a science

---

2. Joseph Carroll, *Evolution and Literary Theory* (Columbia and London: Univ. of Missouri Press, 1995), p. 27.

buff who, even at age ten, had been characterized by his schoolmates as impatient "to learn physiology, botany, geology, astronomy, and everything else."[3] As an adult, it's clear, he was equally eager to impart that knowledge to Christopher Robin and his entire generation. It should come as no surprise, then, that inertial momentum, gravitation, and conservation of mass, which even quite young readers can comprehend, are copiously illustrated by Pooh and his fellow fauna.

Take, for example, *Pooh*'s very first chapter, in which the weighty bear falls from a tree with all the acceleration that Galileo or Newton could have desired—but not, you may rest assured, with a foot per second per second more:

> "Oh, help!" said Pooh, as he dropped ten feet on the branch below him.
>
> "If only I hadn't—" he said, as he bounced twenty feet on to the next branch.
>
> "You see, what I *meant* to do," he explained, as he turned head-over-heels, and crashed on to another branch thirty feet below, "what I *meant* to do—"
>
> "Of course, it *was* rather—" he admitted, as he slithered very quickly through the next six branches.
>
> "It all comes, I suppose," he decided, as he said good-bye to the last branch, spun round three times, and flew gracefully into a gorse-bush, "it all comes of *liking* honey so much. Oh, help!"

---

3. Quoted by Ann Thwaite, *The Brilliant Career of Winnie-the-Pooh: The Definitive History of the Best Bear in All the World* (New York: Dutton Children's Books, 1994), p. 15.

The cries for assistance that frame this remarkably detailed scene, with its proportionally incremental descents of first ten, then twenty, then thirty feet, would be pointless if taken in the sense of "help me stop falling, you who are standing sixty plus x feet below." No, the help in question can only apply to working out a math problem Milne is posing for his young readers and perhaps for Christopher Robin as well. As we see in Figure 1—first slide, please— there are, discounting rotational momentum and the "dead bear bounce" factor, two salient variables here, total distance plummeted and total time of transit from highest branch to touchdown at gorse bush. Since two variables are one too many, the pupil can either stipulate x, solving for T, or stipulate T to solve for x and derive H.

Again, think about the scene, just two chapters later, dealing with Pooh's recursive footprints around a spinney of

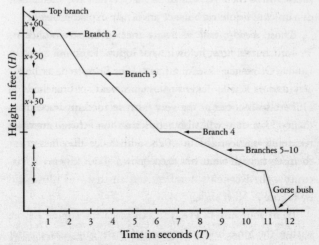

Figure 1. Stochastic teddy bear descent rate.

larch trees. Asked what he is tracking, Pooh pays homage to the difficulties of complex vector analysis when he replies, "I shall have to wait until I catch up with it"—as he never can, of course. The reason why not is hidden from Pooh but not, surely, from a student reader whose synapses haven't yet been switched off by poststructuralism. He or she can readily grasp the tension here between time's forward arrow and the feedback principle that makes possible such counterentropic undertakings as organic life and *Winnie-the-Pooh* itself.

Pooh also teems with puzzles that can engage still older devotees of nature's laws. One instructive example is Eeyore's drifting within the eddies of the stream into which he has been "bounced." Injured dignity prompts the floater to ascribe his motions to free will: "If, when in, I decide to prac- tise a slight circular movement from right to left . . . or per- haps I should say . . . from left to right, just as it happens to occur to me . . . " But fifteen-year-olds who have worked the problems in their physics texts can see that the ineluctable dynamics of liquid turbulence are firmly in charge here.

Those readers will be aware that turbulence—with its Taylor-Couette flow, its Swinney-Gollub doughnut spin, its Landau frequencies measured with laser Doppler interferom- etry, and its Ruelle-Takens one-parameter C^k vector fields on Hilbert space—lies at the very heart of contemporary chaos theory. But they will also recall that the strange attractor remained untheorized in 1928, and hence they'll content themselves with what was then known about kinematic vis- cosity—the Reynolds numbers and all that—as illustrated by Figure 2. Next slide.

If, in your mind's eye, you can place the supine Eeyore within the force lines of segment C here (my laser pointer

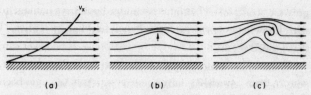

Figure 2. Effect of random disturbance on fluid in laminar flow.

marks the area), you will have grasped Milne's pedagogical intent. Even an eddy, he is saying—nature's laziest-looking, most apparently capricious phenomenon—is deterministic, albeit stochastic and thus not strictly predictable. Egoism and its hastily improvised illusions, such as those that have been paraded before us in this conference, will prove no match for such necessity.

As you can see from the topics and cross-references listed in Handout A, much more could be said about *Pooh* and classical physics. But the relation between science and literature goes far beyond such didactic parallels. As works of art, *Winnie-the-Pooh* and *The House at Pooh Corner* are products of a human organism, a member of *Homo sapiens sapiens*. Whatever that authorial organism thought it was doing in those books, it was also illustrating species-wide tendencies of a lawful kind. For, as Joseph Carroll has irrefutably reasoned, "knowledge is a biological phenomenon, . . . literature is a form of knowledge, and . . . literature is thus itself a biological phenomenon."[4] That is why the great entomologist E. O. Wilson can be so hopeful that, before very long, "even the

---

4. Carroll, *Evolution*, p. 1.

greatest works of art might be understood fundamentally with knowledge of the biologically evolved epigenetic rules that guided them."[5]

Take, for example, the question of artistic form and purpose in *Pooh*. Aesthetic judgment is no effete latecomer to our world; the biopoetic theorist Brett Cooke points out that it's just the most recent consequence of "symmetry-breaking as the early universe cooled."[6] Moreover, artistic novelty recapitulates the choice made when our eukaryotic ancestors two billion years ago "gave up the security of asexual reproduction for the opportunities and risks of sex."[7] Once our forebears had acquired a front end, or "head," thus making a definitive break with jellyfish and starfish, it was only a matter of a few more eons before we would get signs, calls, ritualizations, and finally art. Yet one may read through the entire corpus of trendy *Pooh* criticism without finding a single reference to those momentous developments!

We now know, even if you don't, that art arose in the service of perpetuating genes with a minimum of deadly violence between sexually competing males. It was, and still is, a homeostatic, low-risk solution to the fight-or-flight dilemma confronting suitors. Thus the proximate antecedents of literature prove to have been such formal standoffs as the male stickleback rivalry display, as shown in Figure 3.

---

5. E. O. Wilson, *Consilience: The Unity of Knowledge* (New York: Knopf, 1998), p. 213.

6. Brett Cooke, "Biopoetics: The New Synthesis," in *Biopoetics: Evolutionary Explorations in the Arts*, ed. Brett Cooke and Frederick Turner (Lexington, Ky.: ICUS, 1999), p. 23.

7. Cooke, "Biopoetics," p. 21.

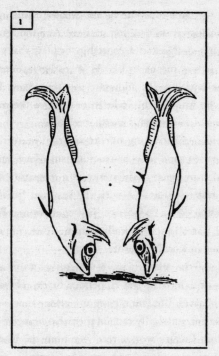

Figure 3. Semiogenesis of art: function as form.

As Walter A. Koch elaborates, "The decalogue of semiogenesis exhibits the *metagenetic primum* as the *genetic secundum* with the *genetic primum* being the ultimate target for epistemic endeavor."[8] But that's not all. More narrowly, we are also looking at the semiogenesis of *Pooh*, a work characterized

---

8. Walter A. Koch, *The Biology of Literature* (Bochum, Germany: Brockmeyer, 1993), p. 11.

by exactly the same topsy-turvy, *now*-what-are-we-supposed-to-do inconclusiveness that you see here. And though *Pooh* is not explicitly designated a courtship display, that's in fact just what it was meant to be. As an earlier speaker mentioned, the book's secret addressee was the actress Leonora Corbett, who was thereby induced to serve as the naturally polygamous Milne's surplus sperm receptacle.

It's almost embarrassing to compare the "gratuitous and obviously false vision" of poststructuralism—"a wrong turn, a dead end, a misconceived enterprise, a repository of delusions and wasted efforts"[9]—with the vast and fruitful perspectives afforded by Biopoetics. Just contemplate Figure 4 [opposite], Carroll's scientifically informed ordering of every major theme in world literature.

If some of the terms here are unfamiliar to you, you'll find them explained in the Appendix to my Handout B, Charts and Tables. But you can see at a glance that there's no limit to the concentrically ranged thematic elements we can locate within literary works, reaching from the whole cosmos—"a very large place," as Carroll has noted[10]—down to the deep interior of the cognitive map.

And the linkage isn't just conceptual but inspiringly physical as well. Since the individual person—for example, A. A. Milne or Christopher Robin—is made up of "organs, tissues, cells, cell structures, biomolecules, atoms, and quanta,"[11] his lowest-level components are literally stardust, and we have in hand a *scientific* rejoinder to those who claim

---

9. Carroll, *Evolution*, pp. 466, 468.
10. Carroll, *Evolution*, p. 238.
11. Carroll, *Evolution*, p. 230.

that there's nothing outside the text. Derrida to the contrary notwithstanding, every quark and gluon within *Pooh*—the paper, ink, stitchery, everything!—partakes of our universe and cries out to be understood accordingly.

Atoms and outer space, however, are not thematically prominent in *Winnie-the-Pooh*. Instead, the world of Piglet and Tigger is tightly enclosed within Carroll's Bios, Antropos, and Polis. Yet this is precisely the fictive terrain where Biopo-etics has accomplished its most impressive fieldwork. Now that we've reached point III.D in my lecture outline, Hand-out C, we can turn our full attention to the very deliberate

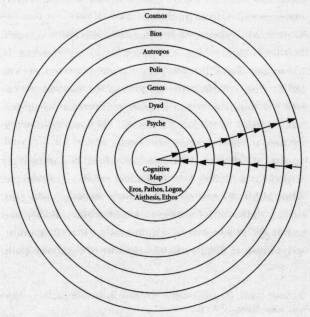

Figure 4. Table of thematic fields and elements.

and instructive Darwinian implications of Milne's plot, which he took pains to situate in a solidly real locale—Ashdown Forest and the Five Hundred Acre Wood—that lay adjacent to his country home at Cotchford Farm, Hartfield, Sussex, England, Earth.

That flood-prone stream, those firs, beeches, gorse bushes, and bogs, that ancient chestnut tree in which Owl has built his nest—all together, these elements constitute a pulsating ecosystem that serves as a virtual laboratory of adaptation and ethology. And Milne not only shows himself to be fully immersed in the Darwinism of his own time; he brilliantly anticipates later discoveries by Robert Trivers, Niles Eldredge, Richard Dawkins, and others. Hence, though some of you probably think there's no relation between, say, haplodiploidy and Hipy Papy Bthuthdy, you couldn't be more wrong.

Construed as representatives of their respective animal species, Pooh and his friends do present the ethologist-critic with one huge anomaly: a singular unconcern for propagation. As Aaron Lynch justly remarks, "The most basic family decision is whether to pursue family life at all. Parental replication favors a widespread yes to this question."[12] Reproductive success, Carroll admonishes us, "is central to human concerns and thus to literary works";[13] and that surely goes double for works containing rabbits. Yet the terrestrial and avian males who form nearly the entire population census of *this* work own neither the physiological

---

12. Aaron Lynch, *Thought Contagion: How Belief Spreads through Society* (New York: Basic Books, 1996), p. 42.
13. Carroll, *Evolution*, p. 2.

apparatus nor the inclination to mate. Quite the contrary. By trivially pleasing themselves in the here and now, our actants exemplify that ominous break with natural selection that Pierre van den Berghe takes to be not just human but distinctly modern: "We proclaim, in effect, that we love the entire assemblage of genes we call 'me' better than our genes taken separately, and that therefore we are going, in some circumstances, to gratify that 'me,' even at the expense of reproducing our genes."[14]

If this sentence can stand as a virtual credo for the nonfornicating playboy and all-around narcissist Winnie-the-Pooh, must we not concede that he has no more hope of descendants than the House of Usher? Those of you who have been waiting to find a flaw in Biopoetics are probably sensing victory now. Once we realize, however, that we're dealing not with individual animals but with types (*the* wise owl, *the* squealy piglet, and so on), we can see that their insouciance about replication corresponds to the stability experienced by whole species in the vast interludes between environmental catastrophes. As Niles Eldredge puts it—and it is difficult to imagine that he wasn't thinking of *Pooh* here—"Species do not play economic roles in nature. They do not have niches. Indeed, . . . species *do not seem to do much of anything at all.*"[15]

Further oddities in the Ashdown menagerie gain coherence when we realize that these animals are not wild but

14. Pierre van den Berghe, *Human Family Systems: An Evolutionary View* (Westport, Conn.: Greenwood, 1983), p. 183.
15. Niles Eldredge, *Reinventing Darwin: The Great Debate at the High Table of Evolutionary Theory* (New York: Wiley, 1995), p. 189; emphasis added.

domestic: their sustenance and safety are guaranteed by Christopher Robin and, in the discreetly obscured background, by his parents. Hence their evolutionary fitness is staked not on their ability to breed and to protect offspring but on their attractiveness to their caretakers. Far from being threatened with extinction by their inability to find their way home through the mist or to tell the difference between real and imaginary threats, they help themselves precisely by being helpless.

The same realization solves another mystery that ought to concern you all: why these representatives of antagonistic species get along so well. Quite simply, it is in their interest as domestic breeds to do so. If the nocturnal raptor Owl refrains from dining on Rabbit's rodent cousins, and if Tiggers prefer extract of malt to surprisingly accessible bears, pigs, and kangaroos, it's because they all make up a quasi superorganism akin to a bee colony. In their artificially controlled biosphere, featuring territorial and caloric bounty for one and all, adaptive tracking has suppressed predation in favor of reciprocal altruism.[16]

The *Pooh* environment is so benign, in fact, that Milne can even suspend William Hamilton's principle of inclusive

---

16. Nevertheless, in prescient anticipation of modern altruism theory, selfishness in the *Pooh* habitat has been merely contained, not abolished—and Milne goes out of his way to make the point. He unflinchingly acknowledges the prevalence of in-group biasing, exemplified by Rabbit's attempts to mobilize his motley herd for a united front against the newcomers Tigger and Kanga. And by-product mutualism is stretched to its limits by the chronically non-reciprocating Eeyore, to whom Rabbit quite reasonably protests, "You've never been to see any of us. You just stay here in this one corner of the Forest waiting for the others to come to *you*."

fitness through kin selection. In the real world, as opposed to the make-believe world of *Winnie-the-Pooh*, kin selection determines just how we must behave in any given emergency. Suppose, for example, a gang of thugs is approaching, and you are tempted to scream. Since your outcry will call attention to yourself and thus increase your danger, you would ordinarily suppress it. But as Lee Dugatkin has shown, kin selection would compel you to scream if you would thereby alert either two siblings, two parents, four grandparents or grandchildren, four uncles or aunts, or eight cousins. A mere spouse, being no blood relation of yours, wouldn't count at all.[17]

Thus if a fire were to break out in this hall, I would attempt to identify those of you who share one or more of my post–Iron Age ancestors and then trample the rest of you (including, regrettably, my husband, George, now seated in row 34) as I headed for the exit with that cherished band. In providing Rabbit with an extensive kin network, Milne sets us up for just such a lesson in genetic triage. When, instead, the relations turn to helping (of all things) an imperiled bear, the author offers his boldest instance of the denaturing effect of domestication.

Could it be, however, that the *Pooh* characters are only pretending to be beasts? No amount of domestication can

---

17. Lee Dugatkin, *Cheating Monkeys and Citizen Bees: The Nature of Cooperation in Animals and Humans* (New York: Free Press, 1999), pp. 44–45. As Dugatkin elaborates, "Consider the case for siblings. If a single sibling hears an alarm call, then $r=\frac{1}{2}$ and b and c are still each $\frac{1}{2}$. In that case r multiplied by b is not greater than c, Hamilton's Rule is not met, and cooperation via kinship is not favored by natural selection" (p. 45).

explain why they employ idiomatic modern English to influence one another and to speculate about places, contingencies, and creatures not yet encountered. Only human beings, as Wayne E. Allen perceptively observes, "systematically engage in, and manipulate, mentally generated conceptualizations for purposes ranging from self-gratification . . . to the extrasomatic symbolic representation of these conceptualizations, oftentimes with the agenda, sometimes hidden, of manipulating the responses of conspecifics."[18] That is exactly what happens every time Pooh or Piglet attempts a ratiocinative vocalization of a drive, need, or apprehension! Furthermore, Milne's chronic procrastinators lavishly exhibit what Derek Bickerton has identified as the defining trait of our own species—the principle that "if you see something that might be important, do nothing right now, think about it, and maybe you can do something later on."[19]

The strongest evidence favoring a human frame of reference is the prominence of *memes* throughout the PoohUmwelt. To be sure, the meme as such was undiscovered in Milne's day. But this is hardly an obstacle, since the whole point of meme theory is to show how those parasitic molecules of mental transmission (formerly called, prescientifically, "ideas" and "devices") work their own will on unsuspecting people. They replicate all by themselves, leaping from one human brain to another and thus substituting cultural for zygotic reproduc-

---

18. Wayne E. Allen, "Biochemicals and Brains: Natural Selection for Manipulators of Sexual Ecstasy and Fantasy," in *Biopoetics*, ed. Cooke and Turner, p. 158.
19. Derek Bickerton, *Language and Human Behavior* (Seattle: Univ. of Washington Press, 1995), p. 57.

tion. Memes possessing various degrees of survivability include the zoot suit, the Great Society, the antimacassar, compassionate conservatism, "Zippity Doo-Dah," God, and "Louie Louie."

Richard Dawkins, whose discovery of the meme has conferred a quasi immortality on the Dawkins meme, provides his own, more generic, list of sample replicators: "tunes, ideas, catch-phrases, clothes, fashions, ways of making pots or building arches."[20] Ways of making pots? One thinks immediately of *Pooh* and its cornucopia of pots—pots of honey, pots once containing honey, pots mutated into a headpiece, a gift box, a boat. In *Pooh*, the pot meme has disdained a mere niche and has instead achieved a reproductive prodigality that we do not see in rival memes until *Invasion of the Body Snatchers*. And many another successful meme, from the umbrella and the birthday party through the spontaneous social call that extorts A Little Something from one's host, can be seen to flourish in the hothouse culture of Ashdown Forest.

But the meme of all memes, not only in the *Pooh* series but just about everywhere, is none other than Winnie-the-Pooh himself. Of course it's indisputable, as Professor Bruno and others have remarked, that Pooh *as a character* is gradually ceasing to be of interest to his superordinate symbiont Christopher Robin. But that character is only one incarnation of the extraordinarily adaptable Pooh meme. Look around anywhere and you'll see that Pooh has made good on

20. Richard Dawkins, *The Selfish Gene* (New York: Oxford Univ. Press, 1976), p. 206.

the Beatles' ill-advised boast of being bigger than Jesus now. The lovable ineptitude that made him initially appealing to his fickle master was cunningly aimed, all along, less at Christopher than at us meme carriers—readers, moviegoers, consumers of copyrighted images—who will keep him alive indefinitely. Opportunistically invading Milne's text and Shepard's drawings long enough to attract the interest of that consummate cultural colonizer, the Disney corporation, the Pooh meme has propagated itself with all the viral ingenuity of the curtain call, the sales tax, or the meddlesome mother-in-law.

By now it should be obvious that the immediate future of literary criticism belongs not to you Luddites and dilettantes but to those of us who have been giving the Biopoetics meme a chance to quicken its march toward academic pre-eminence. In the longer run, however, even Biopoetics will be radically transformed within E. O. Wilson's still grander vision of *consilience*, or the restatement of all knowledge in physicalistic terms. "What we call *meaning*," Wilson has declared, "is the linkage among the neural networks created by the spreading excitation that enlarges imagery and engages emotion."[21] He thus foresees experiments in which responses to literary texts—and why not *Pooh?*—are monitored by "a team of scholars . . . [who have] constructed an iconic language from the visual patterns of brain activity."[22] "In the silent recesses of the mind, volunteer subjects recount episodes, . . . and while they are doing this the fiery

---

21. Wilson, *Consilience*, p. 115.
22. Wilson, *Consilience*, p. 117.

play of their neuronal circuitry is made visible by the tech-niques of neurobiology."[23]

But why stop there? Once meaning has become fully machine-readable, the literary criticism meme may decide that it can do without human interpreters altogether. Just such a change, on a far broader scale, has been predicted by the memetic futurist Susan Blackmore, who looks forward to a day when robots, initially programmed with a sprinkling of memes, may evolve "motivations that we could only guess at" and end by excluding us from their culture.[24] Like the merely physical teddy bear who, at the end of *Pooh Corner*, gets discarded like last year's punctured Hacky Sack, mortal critics will find themselves descending from ecologically secure footholds to endangered status to extinction. At that point, career adjustments will be necessary even for those of us who correctly anticipated how the academic meme pool would evolve. But at least you and I can resolve right now to objectify our interpretative practices so that, when the robots do take over, they will judge our readings to be almost as precise and congenial as their own.

23. Wilson, *Consilience*, p. 118.
24. Susan Blackmore, *The Meme Machine* (Oxford: Oxford Univ. Press, 1999), p. 218.

CHAPTER EIGHT

The Courage to Squeal

DOLORES MALATESTA

Dolores Malatesta is not an academic but a successful practitioner of A. A. Milne's own specialty, stories for younger readers, in which capacity she was invited to join the "Postmodern Pooh" forum as a guest speaker. Small children, however, are not her preferred audience; she writes chiefly for late-adolescents, especially those of her own sex. Typically, her stories are set in her native Pacific Northwest—for example, *Tiffany the Apprentice Tree Spiker* (1988) and *Bigfoot's Daughter Builds a Boeing* (1992).

Malatesta is best known for the trilogy *Vanessa Vernon, Teenage Healer* (1995–1999), the saga of a Seattle high school student who discovers within herself a gift for helping her female classmates come to terms with their drug dependency, their codependency, or in some cases simply their dependency. Readers everywhere, young and old alike, have wept over the concluding scene of the final volume, *Vanessa*

Remembers, in which the young heroine visits her father in prison and forgives him for the crimes against her that he is still attempting to recall.

A teddy bear may be worth more than a father.
                                        —Christopher Robin Milne

THANKS so much, professors, for asking me to join this conference of yours. I've listened with considerable interest to the strange and shocking things you've had to say about *Winnie-the-Pooh*. What's really shocking to me, though, is the way you take its repulsiveness in stride. You aren't bothered by all the excrement and homosexuality and Communism that you dig up; it's all in a day's work for you. Well, I'm hoping to shake you out of such complacency today.

As a mother and a writer, I expect books for children to be full of wholesome instructive values. I believed that *Winnie-the-Pooh* was such a book when I started reading it to my daughter back in the early nineties. Right away, though, alarm bells went off. Every time we got to a part about the character called Piglet, Darlene would start sobbing and begging me to stop—and you can bet that I did, right away. I already knew that when it came to detecting inappropriate goings-on, Darlene was a regular canary in the mine shaft. It was as if she could look straight through the "humorous" plot and see that little Piglet, at the rate he was going, would end up under restraint in a mental ward.

The background to my daughter's moral sensitivity, you may as well know, was the famous Kamloops Wee Wascals case that came to trial in 1989. My former husband and Dar-

lene and I were living in Kamloops then, and Darlene was
the very child who disclosed, one day when I was driving her
home, that those day-care workers were "nasty old meanies."
She was so upset about it that I notified the local police, who
interrogated all of the toddlers over and over with anatomi-
cally correct dolls and with candy treats for truthfulness. As
you probably recall, the entire Wee Wascals staff eventually
proved to be sadists who had savagely molested the helpless
kids with magic wands while wearing clown suits and party
hats with live lobsters on top, reciting nursery rhymes back-
wards, and, as one frightened boy stated in court, "making
funny noises with their poopies."

All of those fiends are safely behind bars now, but Darlene is still dealing with issues from back then. And so am I,
to put it mildly. Darlene's ordeal aroused some suspicions in
my own head, so I found myself a good therapist—in fact,
the best one around, with a 100 percent record of success
in learning the truth about her clients' early years. Sure
enough, after a couple of months of journaling, guided
imagery, dream interpretation, and communication with my
Inner Self Helper through hypnosis under sodium amytal, I
learned that my seemingly normal childhood had been a
hideous lie.

I'm not going into the painful details here. I'll just say
that, following medical advice, I've been obliged to do a par-
entectomy, replacing my family of origin with a family of
choice, my support group of fellow survivors. And, yes, a
husbandectomy proved necessary as well, because when
you've suffered in the ways that Darlene and I have, a scoffing
disbeliever in the house is just as intolerable as a perpetrator.

As you can imagine, I gave *Winnie-the-Pooh* a wide berth
for many years. Once I reread it in response to your invitation,

though, the whole sordid story began falling into place. Following what I'd picked up from Darlene, I started by listening very attentively to Piglet's distress calls. They may have escaped your notice, but they came through loud and clear to me:

HELP!

PIGLET (ME)

IT'S ME PIGLET, HELP HELP.

Now, I understand that Piglet is not a person but an immature pig, and I also know that this pig is only a character in a work of fiction. Technicalities of that sort are all the excuse that most of you eggheads need to overlook the important questions. You hesitate to ask yourselves *why* the book happens to contain a fictional pig who's deeply disturbed. It doesn't occur to you that the author, if he had been feeling all right down inside, could have made this pig into anything he pleased—Porky Pig, Miss Piggy, you name it.

But no, it is a little pig who appears to be borderline anorexic and sorely lacking in self-esteem, as witnessed by his tiny smudge of a signature and a voice whose squeakiness all but spells out *i-n-s-e-c-u-r-i-t-y*. The pitiable creature squeaks HELP HELP and thinks, "So now somebody else will have to do something, and I hope they will do it soon." Somebody will, here and now. Help, or at least delayed justice, is on the way, not for Piglet personally but for the real-life victim whose pain can be heard in his borrowed voice.

Pigs in general, as I'm sure you know, like to wallow in slop and give their full attention to foul scraps of garbage. Not

Piglet, though. Whenever he's approached unawares, he goes
into Ambush mode and gets flooded with what the text calls
"Surprise and Anxiety." He worries that other animals seem
much too big and/or much too bouncy, and he jumps at every
noise. In one significant episode he experiences a suggestively
rhythmical, pounding, up-and-down motion sickness:

> this   take
> "If   is   shall   really   to
>   flying I   never   it."

And even more telling, when he sees a river overflowing its
banks, he wonders "whether it would be coming into *his* bed
soon." Not his house, mind you, but his bed.

All of these facts seem to be connected to something
that's even further out of the ordinary. In a book supposedly
written to help the author's son grow up to be a normal boy,
the bear hero's best friend seems to be headed in the other
direction. Tell me, what would you think if Piglet were a
youngster living in your neighborhood? When he walks by
your house and you hear him singing, the only words you
can make out are "tra-la-la, tra-la-la" and "tiddle-um-tum,
tiddle-um-tum." Other kids are flexing their hormones by
learning to hurl penknives into the dirt, to spit and pee at
indicated targets, and to twist each other's arms—but Piglet
is different. Like Ferdinand the Bull, he's too busy smelling
the flowers. Furthermore, when Pooh hears that a party will
be held in honor of Piglet's rescue from a flood, he betrays his
own concern about his friend's gender identity: "Will there
be those little cake things with pink sugar icing?"

Through the fictional mask of Piglet, A. A. Milne seems to
be obsessing about both nervous prostration and incomplete

maleness, as if there were some deep connection between the two. And what's even weirder, he is addressing all this to his only child. So I wondered: could Piglet's freaked-out girlishness be telling us something about the way Milne thought about Christopher Robin?

Christopher's autobiography, published when he was fifty-four, put me on the right trail of inquiry. At some point, it seems, he had learned that Alan and Daphne Milne were crushed when their expected baby daughter turned out instead to be a boy. They gave him a female middle name, dressed him in smocks through age nine, and allowed his long curls to stay uncut until he was ten. Christopher later recalled that he felt humiliated when strangers mistook him for a girl, and "in my very earliest dreams I even used to dream I was a girl." Also, what he liked to do best of all was sewing and knitting. "I remained a boy," he bitterly recalled. "But only just."[1]

This boy-girl didn't turn out to be gay in later life, but there was something precociously sexual about him. We know it from a reporter named Claude F. Luke, who visited the Milnes and wrote up his impressions of the little angel with "the fair, silky head" and the strangely passive manner. Mr. Luke had to discard his intention of conducting "he-man-to-he-man talk" about rugger and such:

> You see, Robin, quite unconsciously, affects you like
> that, struggle against it as you may. He disturbs any-

1. Christopher Milne, *The Enchanted Places* (Toronto: McClelland and Stewart, 1974), pp. 22–23, 95–96, 15, 38–39, 128.

one who has firmly decided to keep things on a manly plane. . . . And if critics urge that such is dangerous effeminacy, I can only plead that they have not seen that portion of Master Robin's neck where it has risen white and hairless from the light-brown jersey and just before it has drowned itself in the golden shower above.[2]

If "Robin" could produce this meltdown of a gruff stranger's defenses against homoerotic fantasy, how had he learned to be so seductive? I had a hunch that something a good deal worse than cross-dressing must have been forced on him at some early stage of his life. And I also guessed that this experience, if I could only pin it down, would explain why Milne put *two* Christopher Robin figures into his books: one lifelike in form but implausibly contented, even smug; the other a virtual basket case, like his real-life counterpart, but tactfully disguised as a neurotic, emasculated pig.

As a writer who has familiarized herself with mental health topics and who is now in her eleventh year of continuous memory retrieval and rage work, I think I've got some qualifications for getting to the bottom of all this. Of course I can't put Milne or Christopher Robin, much less Piglet, on the analytic couch. But they left behind substantial evidence that any interested reader can examine. And as soon as that evidence is interpreted psychodynamically, it forms a consistent symptomatic pattern.

---

2. Quoted by Ann Thwaite, *The Brilliant Career of Winnie-the-Pooh: The Definitive History of the Best Bear in All the World* (New York: Dutton Children's Books, 1994), p. 108.

What is it, I asked myself, that terrifies Piglet most of all? Unquestionably, it's a single figure, an imaginary but awesome and implacable beast who visits him in his dreams:

By and by Piglet woke up. As soon as he woke he said to himself, "Oh!" Then he said bravely, "Yes," and then, still more bravely, "Quite so." But he didn't feel very brave, for the word which was really jiggeting about in his brain was "Heffalumps."

What was a Heffalump like?

Was it Fierce? . . .

Was it Fond of Pigs at all?

If it was Fond of Pigs, did it make any difference *what sort of Pig*?

Supposing it was Fierce with Pigs, would it make any difference *if the Pig had a grandfather called TRESPASSERS WILLIAM*?

There are several telltale features here. In the first place, we know from E. H. Shepard's illustration that Piglet has experienced a vivid nightmare of being chased by a Heffalump. The hairy monster's enormous extended trunk plainly shows what kind of threat it poses. Yet Piglet doesn't remember having dreamed about a Heffalump at all; *he has repressed it*. The questions he asks himself as he struggles for calm betray the typical uncertainty of a child sexual victim as to whether his abuser is fond or fierce, friend or foe. And the hoped-for protection from TRESPASSERS WILLIAM is an especially revealing touch. Ask yourself who, according to a little boy's way of thinking, might be dissuaded from further "trespass" if the child's *grandfather* could intervene. Doesn't that point to a guilty *father*?

Nightmares like these have only one possible meaning, and now you know what it is. The Heffalump incubus is a sign of early molestation that has been repressed or dissociated in the deepest compartment of Piglet's fractured mind. For, as the Harvard psychiatry professor Judith Lewis Herman authoritatively puts it, "the ordinary response to atrocities is to banish them from consciousness";[3] and we all know that bad thoughts and memories about sex are more likely to be banished than any others.

Of course, some of you may be wondering whether a pig's mind works in just the same way as a person's. Modern scientists, though, have done lab experiments with outcomes that offer reassurance on this point. As Dr. Lenore Terr of the University of California at San Francisco says:

> It is possible to prove how lasting and influential childhood memories can be, in lower forms of life. . . . Using his shock-aversion technique on fruit-fly larvae, Tim Tully . . . has shown that childhood memories last through something as strikingly disruptive as metamorphosis.[4]

Maybe someday researchers will tell us whether those fruit-fly larvae are subject to unwelcome sexual advances from pervert flies in the adult state. But meanwhile, the case of pigs looks pretty straightforward by comparison.

---

3. Judith Lewis Herman, *Trauma and Recovery* (New York: Basic Books, 1992), p. 1. That rule explains why survivors of abductions, concentration camps, and massacres hardly ever recall that something unpleasant was going on.
4. Lenore Terr, *Unchained Memories: True Stories of Traumatic Memories, Lost and Found* (New York: Basic Books, 1994), p. 109.

When the overwhelmed Piglet tries to translate his panic into words, his speech regresses to the age—my therapist says it would be two human years and seven months—at which his molestation began: "Help, help, a Herrible Hoffalump! Hoff, Hoff, a Hellible Horralump! Holl, Holl, a Hoffable Hellerump!" Equally typical of repressed trauma is the displacement of the offending organ upward to the other end of the abuser's body, where it's still subject both to massive negation and to the repetition compulsion: "It had the biggest head you ever saw, Christopher Robin. A great enormous thing, like—like nothing. A huge big—well, like a— I don't know—like an enormous big nothing." And trembling at the thought of yet another nighttime visit from the insatiable brute, Piglet even thinks about resorting to the classic wifely plea for one night off: "But suppose Heffalumps were Very Fierce with Pigs . . . ? *Wouldn't it be better to pretend that he had a headache . . . ?*"

The strongest evidence of Piglet's early abuse, though, is the fact that he doesn't have any conscious memory of it at all. Neither did I, for that matter, when I started my own therapy back in Kamloops. In fact, there were lots of other things about my childhood—being rocked in the cradle, having my diapers changed, and so forth—that I couldn't recapture, and the parts I did recall were routine "happy" scenes. My resistance to the therapist's diagnosis told her at once that I'd turn out to be a survivor. She was following Renee Fredrickson's solid rule: "The existence of profound disbelief is an indication that the memories are real."[5]

---

5. Renee Fredrickson, *Repressed Memories: A Journey to Recovery from Sexual Abuse* (New York: Simon & Schuster, 1992), p. 171.

This is why "Denial; no awareness at all" makes up one item in E. Sue Blume's "Incest Survivors Aftereffects Checklist," compiled to "serve as a diagnostic device for suggesting childhood sexual victimization when none is remembered."[6] And, as it turns out, other symptoms on Blume's list fit Piglet's case too perfectly to be just coincidence. There's "feeling worthless," for example, and "high appreciation of small favors by others." There's "abandonment issues," "creating fantasy worlds," and "having dreams or memories." And there's "inability to trust" or, on the other hand, "trusting indiscriminately," both of which describe Piglet exactly. If only Piglet could have consulted that checklist, or Fredrickson's jumbo one, with its sixty-three symptoms, or the even more famous ones by Ellen Bass and Laura Davis ("Do you feel different from other people?" et cetera), he might have been able to face the awful truth at last. But instead of bringing up memories that could make him whole again, he is doomed to burying and tamping them ever deeper into his mental subsoil.

We who are here today, though, can reverse this process without flinching; and once having glimpsed Piglet's history of abuse, we naturally want to find out who the perpetrator was. Of course the first suspect has to be his father— and we've already gathered some evidence for an indictment of him. But the old scoundrel is absent from the story, so he can't be examined for further signs of guilt. All we can say for sure is that his desertion of the needy youth convicts

6. E. Sue Blume, *Secret Survivors: Uncovering Incest and Its Aftereffects in Women* (New York: Wiley, 1990), p. xvi.

him of having failed to provide emotional and financial support. That's just what we would expect from any male chauvinist pig.

To locate the real villain, we have to remind ourselves who the real survivor was: the unnerved Christopher Robin Milne. His book about himself shows that he had the same abuse-aftereffects traits as Piglet, only worse. He tells us, for instance, that he was a very fussy eater[7]—a quirk that shows up on every checklist as a tip-off to oral violation. Or again, while Piglet only dreams about a stampeding Heffalump, Christopher tells us that he sweated out every night waiting for a dragon to invade his bedroom.[8] And when little "Robin," doubly worked over as a literary character and a sex object, had to face the taunts of schoolmates who sensed that he was missing his maleness, he felt inside himself *a sore place that looked as if it would never heal up.*[9] Judging from the dirty-minded papers that have been read in this room, I take it you don't need any help in figuring out what *that* means.

By now it should be plain who Christopher's dreaded "dragon" must have been. "I have exploited them for my own profit," A. A. Milne once wrote of the *Pooh* animals, "as I feel I have not exploited the legal Christopher Robin."[10] Oh, really? Then why was he so anxious to put down an accusation that nobody had made? "My father's heart," Christopher wrote, "remained buttoned up all through his life"—but I guess some other buttons got undone. The older

---

7. Milne, *Enchanted Places*, pp. 37–38.
8. Milne, *Enchanted Places*, p. 25.
9. Quoted in Thwaite, *Brilliant Career*, p. 137; emphasis added.
10. Quoted in Thwaite, *Brilliant Career*, p. 122.

Milne "saw me as a sort of twin brother" and "needed me to escape being fifty." Although Christopher had repressed his memory of just how that need expressed itself, he did recall feeling that he wouldn't have minded if his narcissistic dad had gone away forever—and now we understand why.[11]

Nevertheless, we're still left with the puzzle of why Milne senior would have wanted to include a secret molestation theme in *Pooh*. One possibility is that he was mining the *Pooh* books with coded threats that would subliminally dissuade Christopher Robin from ever bringing the horror into consciousness and blurting out the truth. If so, it's at least conceivable that he wasn't just an abuser but a *satanic ritual* abuser who, having forced his son into a Devil-worshipping sex cult for multiple exploitation, now had to protect the cult itself from being exposed.

Whether you intellectuals believe it or not, there *is* a clandestine worldwide network of Satanists out there who like to molest, torture, and kill children as a sacrifice to the Evil One. Needless to say, they hide all signs of their doings, even the very existence of the babies that they chop up and barbecue. In fact, they're so good at evading detection that when the FBI, some years ago, tried to authenticate reports of their conspiratorial activities, *not a single trace* of evidence could be found! And it's suggestive, to say the least, that the record of satanic cult activity in Milne's England of the twenties appears to have been very carefully and completely effaced.

Certain elements in *Pooh* and *Pooh Corner* do lend support to the cult connection. We know, for instance, that Satanists

---

11. Milne, *Enchanted Places*, pp. 103, 159, 27.

like to dress up in *animal* costumes and that their still-alive children are "*trained with dolls* so that the techniques of sacrifice and *dismemberment* become increasingly familiar."[12] There you would have a neat explanation for Eeyore's grotesquely severed tail. Or again, Satanists emphasize birthday parties with grisly surprise gifts, such as "a pyjama case with a *teddy bear* on the front," but inside, "the rotting flesh of a dead animal."[13] Maybe that was close enough to Eeyore's strange birthday gifts for the real Christopher Robin to have unconsciously noticed the resemblance and to have feared for his life.

In the final analysis, though, this line of interpretation strikes me as a dead end. We do want to be sure, don't we, that everything we assert about the incestuous pedophile Milne is firmly anchored in fact. The trouble with the "silencing for Satan" reading is that it can't account for the touching portrait of Piglet as a nervous wreck who's suffering from repressed memories of abuse. As we've seen, that portrait bespeaks empathy and remorse, not menace, toward Christopher Robin as the victim of barbaric sexual outrages. It's clear to me, then, that *Winnie-the-Pooh* and *The House at Pooh Corner* sprang from a guilty conscience. Milne shows that he understands perfectly well the terrible damage he has wrought on his son's psyche, and he longs to confess the truth. But since he also fears the wrath of the public and the vengeance of the judicial system, he can't speak out, and the net effect is furtive, inconclusive, and unclean.

---

12. Joan Coleman, "Satanic Cult Practices," in *Treating Survivors of Satanist Abuse*, ed. Valerie Sinason (London and New York: Routledge, 1994), pp. 245–46.

13. Coleman, "Satanic Cult Practices," pp. 247–48.

What a contrast, if I say so myself, with the novel I've just mailed off to my editor! It's called *Fishi*, and it tells the plight of a contemporary brave, adept at both computer science and tribal lore, who finds himself torn between the Inuit and Intuit. Since *Fishi* means exactly what it appears to mean, I'm sure you'll never be holding a conference about it—but that's all right with me. From what I've heard here in Washington, the things that make a book fascinating to you English professors are just the things that an author with a clear conscience wouldn't have put there in the first place. Maybe it's true, after all, that "classic" books like *Pooh* and *Pooh Corner* get their staying power from a pathological struggle between revolting impulses and repentant ones. But if it comes down to a choice between self-respect and literary immortality, so be it: give me self-respect every time.

CHAPTER NINE

Virtual Bear*

BIGGLORIA3

Growing up in Ottawa and Toronto as Herbert L. Dribble, the author of the following paper was radicalized by his participation, as a teenage drummer, in Toronto's punk, rave, and filthy acid techno scenes. His band, Goa Ballistic, opened for such avant-garde groups as Maple Leaf Drag, Orifice Party, and Just Say Oh before it dissolved in 1992. Later, as a University of Toronto undergraduate, Dribble manifested his resistance to conformist pressures by continuing to dress in purple suede and chains and to sport an exact-replica Glen Plake orange Mohawk and an authentic Kathy Acker tongue stud.

---

*Editor's Note: On the speaker's instructions, the hall lights were dimmed during his talk and a continuous strobe played over the podium, while his spoken words were accompanied by taped, surround-sound, MIDI-generated white noise. Professor BigGloria3 wishes to thank the members of his fall 2000 graduate seminar Brain Sabotage for preparing these effects.

Our contributor was still formally known as Dribble when he enrolled in SUNY Stony Brook's New Cinema and Cultural Studies Ph.D. program, and again when he began his teaching career at Syracuse University's innovative Center for the Study of Popular Television. At Syracuse he began to explore the literary-critical implications of online chat rooms and social games. Who is to say, he has asked, that logged-off existence is more real than the digitally pulsating cyberworld? Accordingly, Dribble adopted his favorite screen name, BigGloria3, as his scholarly *nom de plume*.

BigGloria3's published papers include "Peeking Duck," a study of Donald Duck cartoons in their early, frankly lascivious mode, and "Teledildonics: The End of Sex as You Thought You Knew It." He is also known for his unusual and provocative teaching, which has resulted, for example, in the pornosatirical 8-mm film *Rodman's Hot Date with Martha Stewart*, acted by members of his senior honors seminar at Syracuse. Although legal obstacles have kept the movie out of distribution, it has become an underground classic among Cultural Studies conferencegoers. Thwarted in his musical ambitions, BigGloria3 now finds himself coping with the glamour and hassle of academic stardom.

SO this is the great important MLA convention, and right here we have an earthshaking forum on that world masterpiece, *Winnie-the-Pooh*. Oh, brother. You know, some of my grad student pals at Syracuse have been job hunting at these geriatric circle-jerks of yours, even though there aren't any jobs worth mentioning. They warned me that you guys are square, but it isn't true. Uh-uh, you're cubic!

I mean, just look at yourselves. About half of you might be auditioning for bit parts in *Dead Poets Society* or *The Paper Chase*. The rest are trying to look kind of cautiously hip, like a Camry with tail fins, but spare me, puh-leaze. It's a system crash either way. The only person I've seen who knows how to make a coherent rags statement is Sissy Catheter, with that Serious Feminist clit-lit grunge look of hers. And it's no accident that Sissy is the only one of you who has said anything halfway interesting up till now.

Ideawise, most of my "fellow panelists" haven't had much luck trying to disconnect from the oppressive categories they were deconstructing. Just take Carla Gulag, who wasn't quite sure she was entitled to enjoy herself in the late-capitalist economic order. Hello? Earth to Gulag—do you read me? If so, listen to Clint Burnham: "Such terms as command / demand economies or globalization or the 'relaxation' of tariffs are themselves explicit sexualizations of the market."[1] You don't have to choose between economics and erotics; the field itself can be a turn-on if you start right out by treating it as wankware.

What all the content providers have shared is a desperate, embarrassing need to root around and "find" some redeeming features of *Pooh* to hang on to. If you can't say that the microbrain author Milne meant to put those features there, why, then, they must be lying concealed in the "unconscious" of his text. Surfaces and depths, now there's a comb-over concept for you. Through the labyrinth of signification with gun and camera, wow. Nothing could be less postmodern than

---

1. Clint Burnham, *The Jamesonian Unconscious: The Aesthetics of Marxist Theory* (Durham and London: Duke Univ. Press, 1995), p. 195.

those hidden symbols, accessed by a master code and linked to a master narrative. And what can I say, except *Get a life*, to people who still yearn to have their "values" validated by books—the killer app of the 1400s. Sorry, but I see I'll have to treat you like newbies and give you a core dump here.

You remember all the wild gay sex that Sissy Catheter thought she was dredging up from the *Pooh* books. That turned her on politically, because then she could think the characters were giving the slip to the original wizard Milne and his dorky inhibitions. But come on, wasn't she just taking her own turn as Pooh's and Eeyore's ventriloquist? Listen, and I'll show you why this kind of stunt is too easy to tell you anything real.

Under an icon of two little boys from the user interface of *Now We Are Six*, it says:

> If John were me and I were John,
> I shouldn't have these trousers on.

This sure sounds like a prelude to heavy action of the kind Sissy "brought to light" in *Winnie-the-Pooh*. She'd especially like the picture of Twist-off-er Rubbin' as he stares at John's pubis and starts fumbling to unbutton his shirt. But what have we got here—a trapped "signified" trying to make a prison break with our help? Negative. I'm just drawing this stuff from my own mind, and why not? I'm bored out of my gourd with all the obvious, reasonable-sounding things that other people have said about the poem.

I'll give you another test case from a different poem called "Waiting at the Window." Here's John again, and it looks like he's back at it:

James is going slowly on.
Something sort of sticks to John.

In fact, though, that was about two drops of water dripping down a windowpane. If you want to make something else out of it, be my guest—just so you don't call your idea the point of the poem.

The same rule applies to *Winnie-the-Pooh*, which is so easy to jam your own thoughts into that you can do it on autopilot after a while. What does Owl "mean" when he says, "It was hanging over a bush, . . . and it came off in my hand"? And what's the deal in this passage?

"So it does!" said Pooh. "It goes in!"

"So it does!" said Piglet. "And it comes out!"

"Doesn't it?" said Eeyore. "It goes in and out like anything."

The sky's the limit if you cheat a little by leaving out whatever doesn't fit your theory:

"And I would go in after it," said Pooh excitedly, "only very carefully so as not to hurt myself, . . . and I should lick round the edges first of all, . . . and then I should come back and start licking in the middle. . . ."

So Pooh pushed and pushed and pushed his way through the hole, and at last he got in . . . humming to himself in a rather sticky voice . . . a Wedged Bear in Great Tightness. . . . And for a long time Pooh said

only *"Ow!"* . . . And *"Oh!"* . . . And then, all of a sudden, he said *"Pop!"* just as if a cork were coming out of
a bottle.

No problema, amigos. Getting your favorite jollies from
the text is a snap, but when you've finished and are shower-
ing off the slime, nothing has happened that means diddly-
squat to anybody but you. If you can wrap your mind around
that, maybe you'll be out of the Middle Ages at last and
ready to see where we can go from here.

Where we're going is toward revolution; Sissy was right
about that. She knows, too, that it can't be the old Soviet
kind, with tractors and statues and five-year plans to crank
out more vodka or something. Revolution is about changing
people from the inside out, busting them free from authority
and hierarchy. But you've got to start by mellowing your
own self and chilling with the idea that everybody's going to
end up in a different place than you. Not *exactly the same place
or else*, Sissy.

I come at all this from the Cultural Studies angle, and
that's probably why old man Hobbs asked me to facemail
with you at this conference. But I wonder if he knew what he
was letting himself in for. When CS first got started, it was
run by a bunch of elitists, alerting the other snobs to the
menace of trashy popular art forms. They were all going to
pitch in to prevent the mass-taste monster from climbing
out of its swamp and overrunning our lovely, fragile Western
Civ. Well, CS has got more bandwidth than that by now. We
endorse the lowest-common-denominator sleaze, because it
thumbs its nose at high-culture "standards" and brings
everybody down to where they're really at. That's why, like

Burnham says, Disney's silly theme song "now can stand as a class anthem for postmodernism."[2] And it's also why Disney's Pooh, idiotic emoticon smile and all, is teraflops more important than the has-been wack Milne's.

CS morphed into its present radical state when Queer Studies came along and gave it a shove. I don't mean Lesbian/Gay Studies, which very politely says to the hegemonic order, "Say, there, if it's all right with you, do you think you can make room in your prison for two more 'marginalized identities'?" For one thing, queerness isn't marginal. When you add in the kinkier heteros—fetishists, jock sniffers, Jesus freaks, doll collectors, day traders, spankers and spankees—queers are the moral majority for sure. And they don't have a fixed "identity," either. Yo, look at me. I've been strictly a front-loader so far, just ask any of the ladies I hang with, but I'm not "*a*" straight, 'cause I reserve the right to switch-hit whenever I might get the yen. That's queer freedom. *Queer* is just a shorthand way of saying, "Why not?"

Well, when QueerStud and CultStud came f2f, a terrible booty was born. It's *political*, man. In fact, one subspecialty of QueerCultStud, Queer Barbie Studies, is doing to "English" what Mattel's subversive workers did when they slipped Earring Magic Ken past the management.[3] QueerCultStudLitCrit is like those floggings, rapes, and dismemberments that rebellious grrrls take out on their Barbies. If our goal, like Michael Warner says, is to "mess up the desexualized spaces of the academy" as a first step toward realizing "the necessarily

---

2. Burnham, *Jamesonian Unconscious*, p. 192.
3. See Erica Rand, *Barbie's Queer Accessories* (Durham: Duke Univ. Press, 1995).

and desirably queer nature of the world,"[4] then we'd better put in some time queering "classics" like *Pooh*, which some of you still think is full of wholesome lessons dropped there by his nibs The Author.

The question is how are we going to go about it? Sissy's way is to bring over a whole truckload of theory from Paris France and dump it on top of *Pooh*. Then we learn that the animals have fetishes where their wands used to be, or something like that. And this supposedly proves that it's tough being a woman but completely impossible to be a man. I still haven't figured out what's so radical about that.

I take this kind of personal, because you might say some of the stuff I'm wearing right now counts as fetishes. I don't feel any big lack, though. Everything seems to be in working order, and if any of you chicks out there want to find out for yourselves, I've got nothing on the books after about midnight tonight. And besides, why shouldn't anybody have a fetish if they feel like it? Annie Sprinkle's got the right idea:

> I have a vision. . . . Fetish lingerie and sex toys will be freely distributed to all people who want them. . . . Men will be able to have multiple orgasms without ejaculating. Women will have multiple orgasms with ejaculation. People will know how to make love without touching if they choose. It will be possible and safe to make love anywhere you want in public, and it will not be considered impolite to watch. No one will

---

4. Michael Warner, introduction to *Fear of a Queer Planet: Queer Politics and Social Theory*, ed. Michael Warner (Minneapolis and London: Univ. of Minnesota Press, 1993), pp. xxvi, xxi.

care who anyone has sex with, or if they are bisexual, gay, straight, or anything else.[5]

Is that rhizomatic, or what? And it doesn't have a thing to do with the phallic mother or the castration complex or the rest of your garbage in, garbage out theorizing. It's just everybody staying cool and leaving plenty of space for everybody else to mess around and explore.

So what should we do, then, with a stuffy, backward-looking, veddy veddy English book like *Winnie-the-Pooh*? The answer is simple: don't analyze it, just sit down and *rewrite* it to suit your own specs. Wherever you see something retro in the story, change it. That's *empowering*, dude. And it will get more so if you trade your beta-release drafts with other writers who are doing their own *Pooh* spin-offs. The age of the passive, sock-it-to-me reader is history now.

In fact, it's been over for quite a while, though I'm sure that's news to you. Does *fanfiction* ring any bells? How about *slash fiction*? That's the slash in *K/S*—you know, Kirk and Spock in *Star Trek*. Women Trekkies have been writing zine-based K/S porn romances, thousands of them, since the eighties—works like Gayle Feyrer's *Cosmic Fuck* series, which CultStud groupies appreciated almost as soon as they got passed around. "Infinite Diversity in Infinite Combination" is the signature of these mostly straight women,[6] but they stick to gay male porn because it does the best job of

5. Annie Sprinkle, *Post-Porn Modernist: My 25 Years as a Multimedia Whore* (San Francisco: Cleis, 1998), p. 193.

6. That was the motto of a 1988 K/S convention in Houston that Constance Penley attended. See her "Feminism, Psychoanalysis, and the Study of Popular Culture," in *Cultural Studies*, ed. Lawrence Grossberg, Cary Nelson, and Paula A. Treichler (New York and London: Routledge, 1992), pp. 479–94.

yanking their heads out of what they already know. And that's what fanfiction is really all about: disabling the fixed-sexual-identity endless-playback mode.

A lot of slash fiction was pretty vague at first, because the women were just guessing about the acrobatics of gay sex. But now they go to a Web site that was set up just to show them how Kirk and Spock ought to get hosed. And the Web itself has become the main slash medium, with over eight thousand sites doing fanfiction porn—not just with *Star Trek* but with *The X-Files*, *Buffy the Vampire Slayer*, and on and on. They're pushing the envelope every day, with no help at all from professor kibitzers.

The *Star Trek* fandom shows that you don't even have to dislike *Pooh* to start changing it in useful ways. All you need is a personal reason to start word processing. Let's say you're a fatty and you're kind of creeped out by what you've been hearing, yesterday and today, about tubby old Pooh. I'm with you there. How many speakers have said, Yeah, sure, Pooh is on the stout side, *but* . . . he's friendly, or loyal, or lovable, or noble? Even the widebody Orpheus Bruno couldn't deal with Pooh's flesh except as lumps of congealed virtue. Give me a break. The bear is just plain fat, not "over-weight," and there's nothing about his size and shape that needs to be excused in any way. Okay, you agree—but what are you going to do about it?

Well, the first thing is to get yourself up and running with some fat-lib porno mags and videos like *Plumpers*, *Bulk Male*, *Fat Girl*, and *Fat!So?* You'll find a taste for heft treated like what it is—just one more sexual preference, certainly no weirder than having the hots for sallow, pouting, coked-down supermodels with coat-hanger shoulders and breadstick legs. "In fat pornography," says Laura Kipnis, "no one is dieting. . . . Cascading mounds of flab, mattress-size buttocks, breasts like sagging, overfilled water balloons, meaty, puckered, elephantine thighs, and forty- to fifty-inch waistlines are greeted with avid sexual enthusiasm."[7] And when you run across gay male fat porn, you'll see that it's "focused less on soft fat than on bulk: bodies in the 250- to 300-pound range, or, to use the vernacular, the 'teddy bear.' "[8] You heard me: the teddy bear.

Now let your imagination run free. Picture a bulging Pooh three times fatter than Shepard drew him. Shimmying through the woods, he attracts the notice of a comparably huge female bear or maybe a randy male—the choice is up to you. Sniffing rear ends, they start their lumbering foreplay, pawing each other's jiggling flanks and taking turns with semi-mounts as the twin Jell-O heaps collide. Take it from there, O.K.? You'll be writing a better story than Milne's, and while you're at it you'll get your rocks off and do your bit for squashing prejudice.

It doesn't have to be porn, either. Suppose your thing is animal liberation. Of course you'll want to start by killing off the "pet owner" Christopher Robin. Try to work a little animal revenge into it—stalking by lions, trampling by a herd of buffalo, or maybe just mad cow disease. Then you can get busy giving names and marquee roles to all the mice and bugs that Milne lumps together as Rabbit's backup group. It might take you several chapters just getting the

---

7. Laura Kipnis, *Bound and Gagged: Pornography and the Politics of Fantasy in America* (New York: Grove Press, 1996), p. 114.
8. Kipnis, *Bound and Gagged*, p. 114.

names and family trees down right, but so what? I mean, have you ever tried to read the Bible? And you've got all the time in the world, because no one's waiting up to publish your stuff.

So—is fanfiction, including P/P (Pooh/Piglet), a sure bet to be the future of writing? I thought so for a while, but then something bigger came along in the nineties: online social games. All of a sudden, it looked like you could forget about tender romance between Tigger and Rabbit or Obi-Wan Kenobi and Qui-Gon Jinn, because now we were going straight for what everybody really wants, flat-out interactive sex with lots of strangers. And it's true up to a point. This is how I've been spending most of my spare time lately, and it beats the hell out of reading *PLMA*, or whatever it's called. You can all join in, and your gender and personality are completely up to you. You can be tinypeople having tinysex, and yet it's *still writing*—writing that makes every other kind of prose look like it's on call-waiting.

Why go to the trouble, then, of tinkering with plots that have already been made up by "artists" like Milne? Well, it turns out that there actually is a good reason. You see, virtual hookups tend to get clumsy, because without a common story thread, too many people are responsible for the plot, and they're all making it up at the same time. Like Gareth Branwyn says, sooner or later the players are going to lose track of each other:

For example, during an on-line orgy of six partici-
pants, someone with the screen name BethR types:
"I'm climbing on top of Roger104," not noticing that
Roger104 has just stated that he is having sex stand-

ing up, in the corner, with Nina5. To work around this story "violation," Roger104 might type: "Nina5 and I get so worked up, we roll onto the floor. As Nina5 falls off me, the always randy BethR, not missing a beat, climbs on top of me." Then, to totally tidy things up, Nina5 adds: "I begin to make out with BethR and to massage her breasts while she rides Roger104." . . . Interactional "train wrecks" are common.[9]

Until real-time technology can work around snafus like this, cyberdroolers will need some rules to play by. If everybody could back off one step and agree to be object-oriented—tying every move to an image in a book with pictures in it—the train wrecks could be kept to a minimum. And why not *Pooh*? I've already shown you how easy it is to browse the story for MUSH—that's multi-user shared hallucination. You and your URLfriends will find plenty of room in Cyberia for avatars like HenryPootel, Alexander-Beetle4, and SpottedorHerbaceousBackson.

You can call this lit crit or not, suit yourself, but I'm here to say it's what's happening. And you should all feel glad, or at least relieved, since it looks like there's still some use for printed mirror sites—books to you. So download and copy, become a player, or forever hold your piece, which is exactly what you'll be doing if you miss all the first-class action.

---

9. Gareth Branwyn, "Compu-Sex: Erotica for Cybernauts," in *Flame Wars: The Discourse of Cyberculture*, ed. Mark Dery (Durham and London: Duke Univ. Press, 1994), p. 230.

CHAPTER TEN

Twilight of the Dogs

DUDLEY CRAVAT III

Although he holds a Ph.D. in English literature from Harvard University, Dudley Cravat III has made his mark not as a professor of literature but as a monthly journalist. In 1985 he became managing editor of the magazine that gave him his start, *Fundament*, whose borrowed motto, "They shall not pass," promises a tightening of shamefully relaxed cultural standards. One perennial topic in its pages has been an alleged carryover from the anarchism of the sixties to the academic establishment of later years. Cravat's most pungent essays on that theme have been collected in two books, *Malignant Boomers* (1992) and *Triumph of the Shrill* (1999).

Since 1987, Cravat has taken pains to attend every MLA convention as a critical observer, always hoping to detect early signs that anti-American academic posturing, as he conceives it, may be on the wane at last. Each February, in a recurrence that some have likened to Groundhog Day, *Fundament* contains a detailed record of his latest disappointment. In

2000, however, at the request of this volume's titular editor, Cravat was actually asked to address an MLA session and to offer his evaluation of the proceedings. The unlikelihood of a second such invitation lends novelty, we hope, to the following remarks, which were otherwise unsurprising to those conventiongoers who heard them through to the end.

Never have affairs of the mind counted for less. Never have hatred for anything that is great, contempt for all that is beautiful, abhorrence for literature been so manifest.

—Gustave Flaubert

Women's studies is a jumble of vulgarians, bunglers, whiners, French faddists, apparatchiks, dough-faced party liners, pie-in-the-sky utopians and bullying sanctimonious sermonizers. Reasonable, moderate feminists hang back . . . silent in the face of fascism.

—Camille Paglia

Basically, they have no morals.

—R. M. Nixon to H. R. Haldeman, speaking of intellectuals

During the 1960s, it became clear that low-priced, mass-produced bears were not simply affecting the appearance of the new generation of bears, they were beginning to threaten the very survival of the traditional handmade bear.

—Michèle Brown

A S we peer out over this nominally full but culturally exiguous hall, tarted up with the typical hotel-chain mishmash of Target Tudor, Cut-Rate Colonial, and Nouveau Ancien Régime appurtenances, we find ourself gazing into a congeries of countenances that speak silent volumes about the present state of criticism. Some visages, we perceive, are contorted in the permanent sneer that is endemic alike to the comfortably tenured Maoist and to the professional "ethnic" who terrorizes with words while exacting ever greater perks and plunder in exchange for refraining from actual mayhem. Others, zombified by long subordination to those same strutting mountebanks, display what the late, too seldom lamented T. S. Eliot immortalized as "timid apathy with no concentration." They are the Hollow Men, headpieces stuffed with postmodern straw. And still others, the disillusioned, long-suffering, but not wholly defeated ones, wear a look of guarded, wary hope—based, dare one whisper it, on the amazing but incontrovertible fact that a scourge of academic cant has been welcomed into these sanctified purlieus and asked to provide his "take" on the whole dubious shebang.

Much has changed, and all of it for the worse, since we ourself, nearing completion of our Harvard dissertation, "Shakespeare: Beacon of Right Conduct for a Later Age," attended the MLA convention of 1976 and discovered that once-abundant assistant professorships for tradition-minded young scholars had vanished overnight. That was bad enough for a profession already in long decline from its apex of cultivated humanism and *bonhomie*. We couldn't have known at the time, however, that the academy would soon devolve into a veritable Cloud-Cuckooland of meaningless and sinister "theory."

Today the memory of our seeming personal setback is tinged with relief at the close escape. We might almost be tempted to offer thanks to the English departments, not only for excluding us from their rogues' gallery but also, by the continual newsworthiness of their shenanigans, for providing us with the makings of a very different livelihood. But we jest. No thanks are due the salaried subversives who, were it not for our own unthanked efforts, might by now have turned the nation's campuses into official adjuncts of the temporarily dormant Soviet Union.

When your chairman, N. Mack Hobbs, mailed us the invitation to speak here today, our instinctive first reaction was to hold the envelope against a light to make sure it didn't contain a letter bomb. Our next thought was that an ingenious practical joke must be afoot. Ha-ha. How amusing it would be, for nearly everyone concerned, were the despised Cravat to arrive, text and site map in hand, at a meeting room where a Kiwanis Club initiation rite or a reunion of octogenarian veterans of the Ice Capades was already in progress—or, better yet, that he be roughed up by MLA Amazons after attempting, in all good faith, to join their confab on the literary mysteries of the tampon. With some reluctance, however, we abandoned that hypothesis when a *Fundament* intern made some calls and ascertained that the intended trick must be a subtler one.

Not having been born yesterday, we are not so ingenuous as to suppose that the redoubtable Hobbs—the self-crowned king of academic theory-mongering—has suddenly awakened to the deficiencies of Left Bank leftism. His career has included many a mercurial switcheroo, but never, to our ken, a turn back toward forsaken higher values. Think about it.

Why, pray tell, would he get religion at this advanced date? No, the likelier scenario is one of sheer tokenism, a sop cynically tossed to those of us who still believe in the cause of literature. Nevertheless, in an exquisitely chic, big-profile, *bien-pensant* academic forum such as the present one, a chance to register even token dissent is a gift not to be lightly declined.

Speaking of news that isn't entirely bad, one must be grateful that the chosen object of your faint praise and frequent calumny is the immortal *Pooh* series. We know those books to be classics because they have withstood the test of time. Admittedly, less time has rolled by since *Pooh*'s publication than since the appearance, say, of the late-Roman author Theodosius Macrobius's lively *Commentary on the Dream of Scipio*. But the differential in years-of-fond-regard shouldn't be taken as an exact gauge of superior merit. Just as Macrobius remains fresher today than his contemporaries Ausonius and Prudentius, *Pooh* and *The House at Pooh Corner* enjoy a firmer place in mankind's affections than the bestselling children's books of 1926 and 1928, Arthur Bowie Chrisman's *Shen of the Sea* and Dhan Gopal Mukerji's *Gay-Neck: The Story of a Pigeon*. And we may venture to predict that this advantage will be maintained down through the centuries that lie ahead.

What you make of a classic depends, of course, on your pedagogical vision, should you happen to have one. But how many here can even recall that the proper function of higher education was once understood to be the fashioning of a gentleman? As T. Atkinson Jenkins wrote in 1914, in an essay whose very title, "Scholarship and Public Spirit," evokes the chasm yawning between us and those innocent times, "The object of the University . . . is to develop character, to make men."[1] Those were the days when the very names of beloved literature professors—such sturdy triple-deckers as William Lyon Phelps, Charles Mills Gayley, George Lyman Kittredge, Robert Morss Lovett—fairly reeked of the roast beef of old England. We mercifully forbear to hold them up for comparison with the monikers—some too exotic, some too demotic—gracing your program list today.

Back then, college lecturers understood that their role was to supply what Fred Lewis Pattee called an "awakening touch" that would rouse students from materialistic torpor.[2] The professor's resolutely amateur spirit would, in Bliss Perry's words, "penetrate, illuminate, idealize, the brute force, the irresistibly on-sweeping mass, of our vast industrial democracy."[3] We cannot refrain from contrasting that sense of mission with the contemporary mania for such unheavenly specialties as "Women's Studies," "Disability Studies," and "Whiteness Studies." What's next, one wonders—"Human Studies," promoting paroxysms of remorse toward our betters among the arthropods and crustaceans?

Of course, the noisy propagandists for "English" as it is currently (mal)practiced cite the sheer variety of extant schools as evidence of openness, vitality, and "multicultural" diversity. But plural ways of sodomizing poems for the sating of political and methodological lusts hardly add up to

---

1. T. Atkinson Jenkins, "Scholarship and Public Spirit," *PMLA* 29, no. 4 (1914), Appendix, pp. cii–ciii.
2. Fred Lewis Pattee, *Penn State Yankee* (State College: Pennsylvania State Univ. Press, 1953), p. 268.
3. Bliss Perry, *The Amateur Spirit* (Boston: Houghton, Mifflin, 1904), p. 31.

genuine pluralism. As for multiculturalism, no correlation can be found between the name (Lat. 'many farming') and the sordid reality for which it now serves as fig leaf. All that's being cultivated is the hard-earned wealth of unsuspecting tax and tuition payers.

The proof of the pudding, when "diversity" stands at issue, is the degree to which non–politically correct sentiments are tolerated in the gulag archipelago of academic thought reform. Woe betide the incautious freshman who raises his hand to hazard a once incontrovertible truism such as "Columbus discovered America" or a patriotic sentiment like "Remember the Alamo." According to the anti-anti-Communist rainbow coalition now dictating the mono/multiculturalist line, our Pilgrim fathers were mere pow-wow crashers; San Antonio is a suburb of Mexico City; and the rest of our native land ought to be signed over forthwith to aborigines and be transformed into one vast combination sweat lodge and casino, where ecologically brainwashed college girls can wriggle out of their very tight jeans to worship the Great Spirit in mystic pelvic gyrations while their parents fork over what's left of their wampum at the blackjack table. We have read such proposals in the liberal weeklies with our own incredulous eyes.

As you doubtless know, it has been our melancholy duty, year after year, to update the fever chart of your afflicted profession by assessing the effusions produced each yuletide by the Modish Languid Association. There is, of course, scant reason for us to be telling *you* our latest findings, since you are precisely the problem. So many of you have charged our research with arbitrariness and bias, however, that we shall take a moment here to correct the record. The *Fundament* staff works with a strictly objective scale for rating MLA papers. By multiplying a measure of Sheer Awfulness by a degree-of-difficulty factor, we arrive at fine fractional discriminations of Net Awfulness, accurate to two decimal places.

The MLA has shown not the faintest impulse toward self-policing since, at its annual convention of 1993, it ascended to its current high plateau of buffoonery, smut, and treason with such paper titles as "Star Power: Or, How to (De)Flower the Rectal Brain" (9.43) and "F___ Your Gender" (9.61). (The editorial omission here is our own; ladies, or at any rate people shaped like them, are present in the room.) There have, however, been upward spikes of matchless grotesquerie, notably 1998's gem on "Internet sex diaries by tourists returning from Thailand" entitled "How My D___ Spent Its Summer Vacation" (9.87). A ghastly attempt at whimsy, perhaps? We were there; we listened, mouth agape; we fled only when we felt our very sanity hanging in the balance.

After such shocks to the nervous system, we would gladly have forgone the pleasure of attending last year's convention. Ample warning of what lay in store was afforded by the Spring 1999 *MLA Newsletter*, soliciting papers for panels characterized in the following all too imitable words:

> **Postcolonialism and Sexualities.** Postcolonialism and representations of sexualities [including deviant performatives], migration and "miscegenation," transnational sex tourism/sex work, postcolonial feminisms and reproductive technologies, sexualities as suturing the private and national or global public spheres.

**Beauty under Construction: Feminism, Aestheti-
cism, and Bad Hair.** Technologies of the visible,
hegemonized beauty, reinsurgent differences, and bad
looks across ethnicities, nations, sexualities, class.

Do you surmise that we invented this self-incriminating
prose ourself? Guess again. What's that? Your second guess
is that we did *not* invent it? Bravo. Give a robotic academic
enough opportunities to compensate for his inherent want of
brain, and sooner or later he will stumble across the truth.

Only a sense of professional obligation induced us to
attend the 1999 convention and to torture ourself with dis-
quisitions on, for example, "The Oprah Canon" and "Good
Breast, Bad Breast: Productivity, Lactation, Demand." But
here we are a year later, in the glitzy new century, bruised in
spirit from visiting your latest outlandish forums on "Queering the Body Politic" and "Sex: Alternative Positions." Sex,
sex, sex! We are not allowed to purge it from our overtaxed
mind for an instant. Even the papers whose titles cunningly
avoid any hint of the erotic prove, once we begin listening
carefully, to reek with innuendo. And so rapidly has the cultural rot accelerated in the past twelvemonth that we've now
had to start rationing our time, remaining at one Leninist-
pederast session only long enough to mark our ratings sheet
and then hurrying off to three other horror shows scheduled
for the same hour.

These rounds of ours in the linguistic lunatic ward
explain why we have had to absent ourself from most of your
own proceedings in this present forum. But we were unlucky
enough to hear the paper that mercifully ended just a few
minutes ago. You will recall that it was mumbled, amid

deafening and blinding *son et lumière* distractions, by a savagely bedizened and bespangled young personage of indeterminate gender who appeared to be so immersed in the "drug culture" as to have forgotten his or her own name. And though the mumbler's words made no rational sense, the *nostalgie de la boue* was palpable. Mister Gloria, I would imagine, fancies that even "The Teddy Bears' Picnic" heralds some sort of Woodstock in the woods. The sight of such a creature inspires no great hope that "Postmodern Pooh" has advanced humanistic learning any further than did the other theorrheic orgies I was obliged to attend, yesterday and today, in order to sample your parent body's perverse parcourse of postmodern performativity.

Prodded, by our advance copy of Gloria's nothing if not provocative screed, to refresh our acquaintance with the fishy business he called Cultural Studies, we got hold of a volume devoted entirely to fulsomely promoting its sordid cause. Those outgunned professors who once put up resistance to Cultural Studies, one is informed in the editors' crowing introduction,

> are gone, retired or dead. We need not wonder how
> they would respond to the work English department
> students and faculty are doing in the 1990s. . . . What
> is obvious is that in discipline after discipline forms of
> cultural studies analysis are routinely under way that
> would have been wholly unimaginable but two
> decades ago.[4]

---

4. Cary Nelson and Dilip Parameshwar Gaonkar, introduction to *Disciplinarity and Dissent in Cultural Studies*, ed. Cary Nelson and Dilip Parameshwar Gaonkar (New York and London: Routledge, 1996), pp. 3–4.

Indeed. Quite so. Just as I suspected. And as if to rip away the last shred of doubt on the point, these victorious Vandals supply us with a choice example: "In 1996, Jane Juffer . . . published her first article—on the lingerie catalogs issued by the Victoria's Secret company."[5]

Your ears have not deceived you: the apprentice academic priestess cut her intellectual teeth on Victoria's Secret lingerie. Are we, then, now enjoined to withdraw our analytic powers from didactic themes and to focus them instead, as one must perforce suppose, on Ophelia's disheveled slip; on the brassiere that barely contains the heaving bosom of Hester Prynne; on Becky Sharp's too infrequently changed panties; on the bathing costume in which the immoralist heroine of *The Awakening* wades to her death; and on the corset straps hastily undone by the adulteress Emma Bovary as she readies herself for a steamy, sweaty coupling, squirming beneath her lover's pulsing thighs? Seriously, now: should a professor of either sex who wallows in such disgusting thoughts be entrusted with the tutelage of impressionable young adults?

The ever partisan Professor Hobbs could not have meant to arm a cultural watchdog with drafts of your papers, but he evidently forgot to "forget" to do so. The result is that, despite his contrary intention, the incriminating documents have fallen into our hands. In all candor, they read like parodies of academic literary criticism at its worst. Nearly all of them are exactly alike: uncivil, adversarial, monotonous, and redundant. And this is a damning indicator of how "English" has lost its way, for those qualities—incivility,

---

5. Nelson and Gaonkar, introduction, p. 3.

adversarialness, monotony, and redundancy—are just the ones that a real gentleman would eschew at all cost.

The almost uniform impression made by your blasts of poison gas spares me the chore of commenting upon them in detail. Professor Marronnez's limp defense of Deconstruction was arrant nonsense. Professor Dat's Postcolonialism was incendiary nonsense. Professor Catheter's Castrationism? Very dangerous and painful nonsense. But the booby prize must surely be reserved for Victor Fassell's wretched tract, which a moment's reflection reveals to have been utter drivel from beginning to end. Everything about it was dishonest but the aptly chosen brand name "Negotiationism," derived from the Latin *negotio ism neg otium*, or "ism business, not leisure." There you have the death of the disinterested literary amateur encapsulated in a single word.

The spirit of fair play enjoins one to add that two panelists, Professors Bruno and Francis, actually ventured to express misgivings about party-line doctrine. They did so, however, without so much as mentioning *Fundament*'s own voice-in-the-wilderness animadversions, issued with metronomic monthly regularity over a twenty-year span. Nor did they have the courtesy to drop into the *Fundament* suite for last evening's sparsely attended martini reception. Like other prudent conventioneers, these self-portrayed mavericks were doubtless kept away by fear of being spied upon and reported to the MLA's equivalent of the KGB. What can one conclude but that they are just two more opportunists, hedging their bets on the next decade's academic fashion and hoping to accrue to themselves, when the wind finally shifts, the credit that rightfully belongs to others?

You are entitled to be told, after our fruitless search through your conference proceedings for one scrap of useful knowledge, how we ourself would propose to interpret *Winnie-the-Pooh*. The answer is as plain as a Marxist agitator's face: we simply dispense with all "theory" and accept the work just as it is. The characters' well-trimmed fur and feathers, their diffident and tactful manners, their geniality and community concern all attest to the author's transparent aim, that of imparting Western Values to a conservatively attired little lad of sound English stock.

Moreover, the educational adventure is meant to be shared by other children. Therein lies the book's not inconsiderable social utility. Children are, after all, not a breed apart but merely very short people whose self-control and range of allusion still want improving. *Pooh* tells us that our democratic cultural tradition—derived from authors probably unknown to you, such as the ancient Greek philosopher Plato and the early Renaissance Florentine poet Dante Alighieri—is accessible to any child, even one born with the admittedly grave handicaps of poverty and ethnicity.

A small number of you, we feel sure, accept the truth of this analysis but dread its application to the classroom, where forty-nine minutes out of fifty would remain after everything of importance had been stated about *Pooh*. How can one teach a work that teaches itself? But the wisdom of a better age could come to your rescue here. More than a century before touchy-feely pedagogy became the norm, professors took literary meaning for granted and trained their students in factual recall, as in these examination questions about the sixteenth-century English poet Edmund Spenser:

> In whose reign did he flourish? Repeat Thomson's lines. What is said of his parentage? What does Gibbon say? How did he enter Cambridge? What is a

"sizer," and why so called? What work did he first
publish? . . . What does Campbell say of Raleigh's
visit to Spenser?[6]

It would not be insuperably difficult to adapt this drill to the
life and times of A. A. Milne. But if you hanker for more
modern and textually involved ways of keeping your students from nodding off, you could consult with profit the
Questions and Study Projects to be found throughout *The
Pooh Perplex*; they remain no less stimulating today than they
were in 1963.

Prior to any large-scale reversal of our universities' sickness unto death, however, a healing impulse will have to
arise from within the academy. Whence, precisely? Thirty-
five years have passed since the "cultural revolution" that
saddled us with obscenity and ignorance in the guise of
spontaneous, androgynous swinging, "teach your parents
well," and strawberry fields forever. Yet the same smelly bare
feet that once trod the litter-strewn encampments of violent
"peace" rallies, thuggish "concerts," and damply groping
love-ins are now wedged into designer sandals and arro-
gantly propped on desks at the head of college classrooms.
Unbiased historians will one day make it clear that Huey P.
Newton and Jonathan Culler, Abbie Hoffman and Geoffrey
Hartman, Janis Joplin and the Beatnik criticess Susan Son-
tag were all engaged in the same fervid *devoir* of Moral Disar-
mament, which continues apace today.

---

6. Charles D. Cleveland, *A Compendium of English Literature* (Philadelphia:
E. C. and J. Biddle, 1857), p. 765.

No one should imagine, finally, that we have taken pleasure from pointing out these hard truths. We have been aware from the beginning that our efforts would reap nothing but abuse from the assembled jet-set egalitarians and from the fawning sycophants who aspire to inherit their thrones. Let the customary sneering and slandering commence, then. And do not, by all means, abate your anathemata simply because today happens—just happens—to be our birthday. We were not expecting any presents anyway, but if you should take a notion to pelt us with tomatoes and rotten eggs, we will try to interpret them not as missiles but as missives conveying—and in turn soliciting from ourself—many happy returns.

CHAPTER ELEVEN

You Don't Know What Pooh Studies Are About, Do You, and Even If You Did, Do You Think Anybody Would Be Impressed?

N. MACK HOBBS

No literary critic, not even Victor S. Fassell, began his career more brilliantly than N. Mack Hobbs, and no one else, from the seventies until now, has so consistently supplied the field with leadership and productive controversy. His has simply been the smartest mind on the critical scene. Although his fundamental and daring innovations of theory always meet with initial resistance from traditionalists, sooner or later the profession tags along like a puppy on a choke chain.

One of Professor Hobbs's startling proposals has been that academic success should be gauged by the same measure as success in the business world; use of any other yardstick is sheer hypocrisy. Tell me your salary, he has said, and I'll tell you your exact place in the serried ranks of intellectual merit. His own rise, through rapid promotions and changes of campus, to his standing as America's highest-paid humanities professor is narrated in an engaging autobiography, *Soldier in the War on Poverty*.

Professor Hobbs's other book-length publications include *Donne Undone*, his early challenge to conventional notions about the Metaphysical poets; *The Last Theory Book You'll Ever Need to Read*, announcing the death of literary theory; two later volumes in the same vein; and his exhortation to college teachers to look out for their own interest, *Still Driving That Old Corolla?* At the time of delivering the following talk, Hobbs was Trustees' Portfolio Tracking Stock Professor of English at Princeton University.

GREETINGS, *Pooh* groupies, theory fans, and humble seekers of a rung on the ever more elusive academic ladder. Hobbs here, as if you didn't know. I hope you've enjoyed these sessions that I put together for you by exercising some friendly persuasion with other movers and shakers in our field. If so, you may want to pick up some souvenir programs that I've autographed for you and left on a table by the door. I thought you might want to frame a memento of the best damn conference you'll probably ever attend. I myself feel kind of sentimental about it, as you'll see.

But first, I know you must have been disgusted by the vile diatribe just concluded. Who is this Dudley Cravat anyway, you must be asking, and who let him in the door? I must admit that the man appears to be an outright racist, sexist, and homophobe. And that's not the image of itself that the Modern Language Association wants to put before the world, is it? Believe me, it wasn't any self-immolating idea of "academic freedom" that prompted me to impose this right-wing fanatic on our valuable time. I was trapped into promising that I'd let Cravat do his Dudley-One-Note routine here today.

Of course, repudiating everything Cravat stands for doesn't mean that we automatically reject all of his judgments. I share his view, for example, that *Winnie-the-Pooh* is a true classic. But that's not because it's chock-full of "Western Values," for God's sake. A classic is just a work that keeps on facilitating professional discourse production. *Pooh* fills the bill, because nobody, not even yours truly, has mapped all of its ambiguities, contradictions, and trapdoors for the unwary.

Until recently, in fact, I hadn't even tried to do so. But then this senile don out in California—the same geezer who stuck me with Cravat—put me onto the *Pooh* series. I started doing some reading in and around those books, and I liked what I saw. I even liked A. A. Milne, especially when I realized that all of the biographical *Pooh* criticism I could lay my hands on had his personality completely backward. When I see that all previous commentators have been played for suckers, it always brings out the teacher in me.

The real expert on Milne was his son, Christopher Robin, who tried to respect him but came to hate his guts and finally wanted nothing to do with him. Christopher eventually perceived, and said in his autobiography, that Milne looked down on the whole human race and had no use whatsoever for children, whom he regarded (correctly, by the way) as egotistical, cunning, and manipulative beyond their years. Anyone not blinded by mushy protectiveness toward his own lost childhood ought to have seen that Chris was right about his father. Milne explicitly stated that he was "not inordinately fond" of children and that he scorned the idea of "tossing off something that was good enough for the kiddies."[1] We've got a ruthless, cynical author here—my kind of guy, and the only kind who can put enough layers of complication into his text to make it worth our critical while.

Other speakers have noted how Milne repeatedly teases us about what is and isn't real, but his radical perspectivism goes deeper than anyone has suspected. His characters don't interact; they collide like bumper cars. Eeyore's "reality" is wholly governed by melancholy, Piglet's by timidity, Owl's by pedantry, Kanga's by maternal feeling, Tigger's by exuberance, Pooh's by narcissism, and Rabbit's by authoritarianism. The cage of solipsism is locked tight and the key has been thrown away. And this leaves Milne, the master of revels, free to pit everyone's illusions against everyone else's while making no commitments himself.

Pooh works flawlessly as a comedy of errors for five-year-olds, but it's also a hall of mirrors whose intricacy bears comparison to the best of Conrad, Kafka, Borges, and Pynchon. Milne tells us the story of his telling the stories to Christopher, who is hearing himself represented in those stories as an omnicompetent resolver of plot entanglements—when of course it's only Milne (subtle mocker of his only child) who plays that role. The author lets each of his audiences—the fictive Christopher, the real one, children, and us adults—see only as much of his intent as he thinks we can handle.

Thus Milne simultaneously flatters, delights, and controls his *actual* son; he ducks responsibility for shaping his *fictive* son's animated nursery, which seems from the latter's

---

1. Quoted by Christopher Milne, *The Enchanted Places* (Toronto: McClelland and Stewart, 1974), p. 13.

perspective to be simply given; he gives young readers tales they can grasp on their own level; and he extracts a knowing chuckle from us, his fellow parents, by making us his tacit accomplices in the art of puppet-string child rearing. And he does it all with an air of transparent, spontaneous ease, thereby reinforcing the real point of the book: his superiority to everyone concerned. The more insouciant he appears while pitting all against all, the more remote he becomes, absconding into the icy outer reaches of that realm where Stephen Dedalus's creator-God sits paring his fingernails, indifferent to his creatures' petty deceits and follies.

Were you impressed by that tour de force of meta-analysis? I thought it was pretty good myself. In fact, I'm afraid it was a cut above anything my colleagues in this forum, including the lifelong *Pooh* "experts," have managed to put forward. I'm grateful for their contributions, of course, but since I subscribe to the Al Davis philosophy of criticism—"Just win, baby!"—I'm even happier to observe that there's still an intelligence gap between N. Mack Hobbs and the rest of the herd.

Because nothing I can tell you will narrow that gap, I don't mind explaining where most of my fellow panelists went off the rails. The problem was left-wing puritanism. Of course there's nothing wrong per se with being on the left; I myself am all for multiculturalism, affirmative action, and the rest of the progressive agenda, which has never posed much of a threat to my career. But it's something else again to fault *Pooh* for not coming up to your partisan standards. All that the professorial Roundheads and Jacobins can do is to call Milne names or—an equally crude ploy—try to snatch his books away from him by "methodologically" improving their politics. The trouble with both alternatives isn't that they're wrong; there's no right and wrong in criticism, only smarter and dumber. But ideologizing is always dumb. It cramps your style, foreclosing the behind-the-back dribbles, the no-look passes, and the alley-oop reverse jams that could put some soul in your critical game.

I have to laugh, too, at the idea that activist criticism of *Pooh* or any other book is going to strike a blow for freedom and equality. It can't bring the world one inch closer to the socialist utopia that constitutes the bleeding-heart professoriat's collective wet dream. Quite the opposite, in fact. Every time you make a contribution, however "radical," to academic chatter, you're playing the established tenure-and-promotion game and thereby strengthening the status quo. That's perfectly fine by me; it's just too bad that I'm the only critic who's frank enough to face it.

If you liked my overview of *Pooh*'s layered effects as much as I did, you probably think that after many false starts we're now approaching the truth about the book. But there you go again, trying to make things simple by ruling out every interpretation but one. All I claim for my reading is that, like a beautiful woman, it's got curves where you didn't know there were places. Of course it's convincing to me, but why should *you* sit there and swallow it? Your role isn't to second my opinion but to crank out some analytic prose of your own—preferably something very different, so that the presses can keep humming and we can all (well, most of us) retain our jobs and keep making the conference rounds.

I dealt with this issue of plural perspectives head-on when I had to serve my term as Princeton's appointed chair of English. Right off the bat, I cold-shouldered the department's old-line humanists, gutted its strict historical requirements, hired specialists in every current fad, and allowed the curriculum to bloat until it included soap operas, Looney Tunes, muscle magazines, bubble-gum cards, and graffiti. Do you think those were predilections of my own? The bumper sticker on one of my Porsches says, "I'd rather be teaching *Hamlet*." But you gotta do what you gotta do if you want your academic unit to be everybody's buzz, and the same rule applies to the field as a whole.

In any case, if I were to advance serious truth claims about *Pooh*, I'd be backing off from another truth claim that put me in the limelight long ago: the dictum that nothing about literature can be known with any certainty. I'm sure you haven't forgotten my most influential essay, the loved/ hated "Lincoln Loggerheads." By attending closely to the opening words of the Gettysburg Address, it showed that no constraints oblige us to read the "Four score and seven years ago" sentence in the threadbare way familiar to civics classes. Why can't we parse "score" as a verb? Then the line could be refigured as having been spoken in chorus by four six-year-olds whose fathers *conceived* them in libertine *liberty* seven years earlier when the latter got lucky ("Four score") after a wild fraternity party. That wasn't what I actually believed about Lincoln's message; the point was that even the craziest reading can't be logically excluded on the basis of textual or even extratextual evidence.

Here, my friends, we've arrived at the inner sanctum of critical postmodernism: there's no such thing as evidence for a reading. Evidence, like theory, is just publicity for a stand already taken. And for that matter, literature itself exists only insofar as we critics constitute it as such, cordoning off certain clumps of squiggles as aesthetic objects. Just as there's no real neutrality and no freedom from preconceptions and no relativism-in-practice and no collective progress in approximations to the truth, so there's not even a literary work to examine until you and I have started trying to explain it.

This is why I consider our forum to have been a true *postmodern* success. I assembled for your edification eleven seductively argued but incompatible takes on *Pooh*, including my own. As BigGloria3 pointed out, most of the panelists hadn't quite given up on criticism's obsolete goal of "determining the text's meaning." But when you try to add up their various findings, presto! the "work as it is" simply disappears. And that's a very good thing. It's time for all of us to concede that there's no stable object out there waiting to be correctly interpreted. Then we can kick back and acknowledge that we're in this criticism racket together, not for the sake of "truth" but just to earn a meal ticket by tooting our little horns.

Of course, some true-believer empiricists will still be unprepared to take that necessary next step. It was amusing but pathetic, for example, to listen to Renee Francis giving us her "evidence" that Milne was the 1926 prototype of Bill Nye the Science Guy. Dolores Malatesta, too, spaded up heaps of "evidence" that Milne was an incestuous monster. Francis chose to overlook the contrary "evidence" that Milne's schoolboy enthusiasm for science and math, in his son Christopher's words, "burnt itself out" long before *Pooh* was written.[2] And Malatesta didn't want us to learn that Christopher and his "perpetrator" father were fairly close friends for a while during his teenage years.[3] But why bother

---

2. Milne, *Enchanted Places*, p. 121.

3. Milne, *Enchanted Places*, p. 122.

pitting "evidence" against "evidence"? If you prefer my Milne to Francis's and Malatesta's, it's just because I'm higher on the totem pole than they are and have a few more rhetorical tricks up my sleeve.

Rhetoric, in fact, is all that's left when postmodernism has done its job of showing that all "knowledge" is socially constructed. Knowledge is simply what the powerful want the powerless to believe—and that gets accomplished through rhetoric. Not even Francis's beloved physical science earns exemption from the rule. You may once have believed, for instance, that the DNA molecule possesses a certain eternal structure that was definitively revealed by Watson and Crick. But as the science-as-literature specialist Alan G. Gross has shown, "the sense that a molecule of this structure exists at all, the sense of its reality, is an effect only of words, numbers and pictures judiciously used with persuasive effect."[4]

Gross places *The Double Helix* squarely within our own field, allowing us to begin speculating—as one critic already has—that the punning title ("double he-licks") of Watson's "nonfiction novel" may point to a sexual relationship between the "base pair" of protagonists.[5] Who's to say that this is wrong, and on what grounds? The quark and the Snark are in the same boat now, and the boat belongs to us.

When good old boys like Cravat hear the news that almighty Empiricism is over now, they go into a predictable panic: mere anarchy is loosed upon the world! But did our

---

4. Alan G. Gross, *The Rhetoric of Science* (Cambridge: Harvard Univ. Press, 1990), p. 54.

5. John Limon, *"The Double Helix* as Literature," *Raritan* 5, no. 3 (1986), pp. 26–47.

orderly sequence of learned *Pooh* papers, delivered with the usual decorum, sound anarchic to you? Cravat thinks that we can't escape chaos in literary study unless a priestcraft of meerschaum-puffing professors transmits precious ancestral sacraments to obedient novitiates. Baloney. The absence of any basis for adjudicating critical claims simply means that a few strong leaders will step in to call the tune. We "super-stars" against whom Cravat ritually rails are the top block of a solid academic pyramid, directing steady lines of force down through the rest of it.

What, then, has *really* changed since the age of those poseur-professors—Kittredge, Phelps, and the rest of them? Quite a bit, but it's all been to the good. For one thing, you no longer need to be a male with a WASP pedigree in order to address "the tradition." And for another, we've given up on untenable mystification about the spiritualizing effect of books. The fashioning of a morally superior gentleman? Well, some of the gentlemen who gave us slavery, genocide, and the hydrogen bomb were steeped in classical literature, while others weren't. It made no difference whatsoever. Today, we're finally able to admit that no poem or novel ever stopped anybody from pursuing his interests and passions, however low.

And speaking of passions, something else has improved in the conduct of our field: the relation between sex and scholarship. A typical English professor in the period that Cravat romanticizes would have had a harem of permanently fixated student devotees who thought they were being touched by greatness, whereas they were just—in both senses of the term—getting screwed. The intergenerational banging is still going on, of course, but it's not so hierarchi-cal and unidirectional anymore. "I learned and excelled; I

desired and I fucked my teachers," writes one eminent literary theorist, recalling her happy years as a Ph.D. candidate.[6]
And now that she's considerably older and holds a distinguished chair, "graduate students," she has declared, "are my
sexual preference."[7] Isn't it healthier to have this out in the
open, where either party can take the lead without romantic
misconceptions or long-term neurotic attachments?

Sex and scholarship: in a twenty-first-century literature
department, it would be hard to say where one ends and the
other begins. You must have noticed, in our conference, that
one speaker after another tried to cut through the pious fog
about Milne's transcendent value system and bring forth the
kinky erotic obsessions that supposedly made him tick. This
recent quest for the author's "core phantasmatic" is both
more ambitious and more inexhaustible than the quaint old
concern with the "organic unity" of individual works.

Kaja Silverman, for example, has proposed that Henry
James's core phantasmatic was "the desire to be sodomized
by the 'father' while occupying the place of the 'mother,' and
the desire to sodomize him while he is penetrating the
'mother.'"[8] But Eve Kosofsky Sedgwick respectfully dis-
agrees. James's *real* favorite fantasy, she has countered, was
the more autotelic and politically untroublesome one of
sticking his fist up his own rectum.[9] And still another critic,
impressed by Sedgwick's analysis, says that he can "picture

6. Jane Gallop, *Feminist Accused of Sexual Harassment* (Durham and London:
Duke Univ. Press, 1997), p. 42.

7. Gallop, *Feminist Accused*, p. 86.

8. Kaja Silverman, *Male Subjectivity at the Margins* (New York and London:
Routledge, 1992), p. 173.

9. Eve Kosofsky Sedgwick, *Tendencies* (Durham: Duke Univ. Press, 1993),
pp. 73–103.

James's head hovering over a consummated toilet, a glossy, smooth turd lolling in the waters, pride summoning lost pleasures."[10]

Here we have a perfect instance of that continuing cultural conversation that Richard Rorty has found to typify the humanities at their best, once we've dispensed with old-fashioned scruples about "evidence" and "plausibility." What does it matter if the core phantasmatic is itself a mere phantasm, invented to keep the critical ball in play? As Rorty has said, if we can just keep talking, we'll be much less likely to slit one another's throats. The show must go on, and it will. As criticism merges with psychoanalysis at one end of the authorial subject and with stool analysis at the other, James, Milne, and every other literary patient can be assured of unceasing and ever more inventive diagnostic attention.

The attention, however, won't be coming from N. Mack Hobbs. I've put my pragmatic stamp on our field, and by now you've learned your lessons well enough to venture forth without my guidance. Indeed, critics like Silverman and Sedgwick have brought the discipline to a point of post-modernity where even Hobbs himself is beginning to look a little traditional. In short, it's time to get out of town ahead of the posse. Besides, I've recently been presented with an offer I couldn't re-use: I'm going to be joining the University of Southern California as vice-provost. Don't worry, I'll still be pushing all the latest trends, however strange—but

10. Renu Bora, "Outing Texture," in *Novel Gazing: Queer Readings in Fiction*, ed. Eve Kosofsky Sedgwick (Durham and London: Duke Univ. Press, 1997), p. 97. The passage continues: "Perhaps it 'passed' (a favorite James term) too perfectly. Perhaps it was less than slippery, and he gripped it within his bowels like a mischievous boy, playing peekaboo with the exit, hiding it upstairs, clinging to it as to a departing lover" (p. 97).

now I'll be doing it for *all* of the humanities. And of course I'll be recruiting headline names for the faculty so that the university can make a big upward move in the charts.

I'll miss all of you English colleagues. You've been a big promotional help to me over the years—especially those of you who've joined Cravat in calling me a dangerous radical and an enemy of reason. That's celebrity that money can't buy. As for *Pooh*, we've probably heard enough about it to last for a while. Still, I'll think about the book from time to time while I'm funding conferences and institutes, hitting up rich USC alumni from the glorious O.J. days, and closing signing-bonus deals with some of the very hotshots you've heard on this panel. You probably won't see me again at the MLA, but remember: somewhere a Bear and his Best Critic will always be playing.